founder vs *investor*

founder VS *investor*

THE HONEST TRUTH
ABOUT VENTURE CAPITAL
FROM STARTUP TO IPO

ELIZABETH ZALMAN
VS **JERRY NEUMANN**

FOREWORD BY SANDY LERNER

HarperCollins
Leadership

An Imprint of HarperCollins

Published by HarperCollins Leadership, an imprint of HarperCollins Focus LLC.

Cover design by Marty McCall

ISBN 978-1-4002-4280-1 (eBook)
ISBN 978-1-4002-4276-4 (HC)

Library of Congress Control Number: 2023931458

Printed in the United States of America
23 24 25 26 27 LBC 5 4 3 2 1

Founder Dedication

To all founders: Whether the knife stabs you in the front or the back, this book is here for you.

Investor Dedication

To all the VCs out there, struggling to make the world a better place . . .

Just kidding.

To my mom and dad, who always gave me the room to make my own mistakes . . . and were there to help nurse the bruises afterward.

CONTENTS

A NOTE FROM THE AUTHORS

In the fall of 2021, Jerry wrote a blog post called "Your Board of Directors is Probably Going to Fire You." The article reached the top of **Hacker News** and crashed Jerry's web server. Founders loved it. Venture capitalists hated it. It had clearly hit a nerve. Liz called Jerry, wondering why anyone hadn't written something like it before. "It's not like things like this are a secret." And so this book was born.

When we asked friends and business acquaintances to read drafts of the book, we got plenty of feedback and tried to incorporate as much of it as possible. Some of it, though, was criticism by founders of Jerry's positions and criticism by investors of Liz's positions, both of which got to the very core of what we were trying to accomplish.

Investors thought depicting the founder/VC relationship as adversarial was wrong and beside the point. They believed both parties should share in the same goal: making the company successful so that everyone makes money. It's never personal; it's strictly business, they said.

Founders wanted the book to have more exposition on how VCs can be coldhearted and counterproductive because investors don't seem to understand or even care how important the founders are to the company and the company to the founders. The founders *are* the business; there is no separation. If investors want the business to be successful, they can only achieve that through the people running it.

This book is unusual, perhaps singular as a business book, because it does not take a side; it takes *both* sides. Not taking a side is the entire point. Founders need to understand that VCs have a job to do. VCs need to understand that founders will never step back and treat the company they birthed as just an investment of their time.

Why should I care, you may ask? Why should I try to understand the other side? It's because when tension appears—in fundraising, in **board meetings**, in growth mode, when facing problems, and when selling the company—those are the moments that can break everything. We've seen it happen. It's happened to us. This book will help you understand it better.

We are also not unusual in what we believe; we're just being intensely honest about it. In fact, we've had some of the biggest arguments of our twelve-plus years working together while reading each other's writing for this book. Yet somehow we've still managed to publish it. And that's the point: You can't avoid disagreement, you can only manage through it.

Whether you're the founder or the investor, you're going to have to talk to each other every week for the next ten years. That's at least one startup trope that's true: It really *is* going to be ten years. Wouldn't it be a whole lot easier if you actually understood the person you're working with?

Enjoy the book,
Liz and Jerry

FOREWORD

It's cold comfort to have survived a mental and financial mauling by the Greediest of the Greedy. In fact, I was taken in, taken by, and fired by the same genius who fired Steve Jobs, an award that—even today—helps soothe the sting. In my case, the ol' divide-and-conquer ploy did not work. In the 1980s, it would have been pro forma to label any businesswoman "not a team player," "too emotional," or "not suited to a business environment." However, they did not ever imagine that Len Bosack, my co-founder, would walk out with me for the simple reason that he felt my being fired was simply wrong. (It's a tactical ploy that founders can use to their advantage: There is no concept of ethical behavior in the Venture playbook.) And, this was months into a strategy to play to Len's masculine ego to keep him onside when the axe fell. His loyalty to me was the only reason that I could keep my stock three years into working for the company (with no salary) and saddled at the time of funding with a four-year vesting agreement that subtly failed to include an employment contract.

Maybe it's nice to know that it could not have been worse, but it's much nicer (not to mention healthier) to not have to go through this painful process. My subsequent ventures were sans mauling, courtesy of my not needing Someone Else's Money. However, if you do need to go to the poisoned trough, I have two suggestions: Get your own lawyer and then read this book.

I'm glad someone has finally written a Guide to Venture Money for the uninitiated, clinically optimistic, and terminally naïve. *Founder vs Investor* is also a lot cheaper than the cost of decades of analysis to help you realize that it really wasn't your fault. Venture money is portrayed as a partnership during the courtship, but founders need to realize that the relationship is wholly adversarial. Venture Vultures not only regard the original team as expendable but—even before the check has cleared—are working to divide, conquer, and claw back the stock. The authors pick apart the lies and illusions, explain the game, and—for the first time—give entrepreneurs a fighting chance to go along with the check.

Founder vs Investor is a practical, tactical defensive handbook for those venturing into the shark pool for the first time and for those who have already been scarred and are wondering what the hell happened. The authors are uniquely qualified to write this exposé: First, they include a woman in a part of the world that is notoriously one-sidedly male, usually behaving badly, and especially badly toward non-males (the stories I could tell you . . .). Second, they have worked both sides of the aisle, as VCs and as founders, and survived. However, what is really remarkable is that they are willing to talk about the process—honestly and—what is better—completely: no pulled punches, no half-truths, no politically correct weasel words. It's a good thing they are successful on both fronts, as I doubt that the Old Vultures' Club is going to be rolling out the welcome mat again. Ever.

Sandy Lerner

1

FEAR, TRUST, AND MAKING MONEY

This book is meant to be the honest truth about startups, but there isn't one truth: Founders and investors sometimes see the world differently. So instead of the two of us writing something we could both agree on, which would be boring and tell only half-truths, we are going to switch back and forth, telling you how we each see the world.

Sometimes we agree, but often we disagree. We say diametrically opposed things. That's the point. Sometimes one of us will emphasize something the other downplays. That's also the point. We want you to hear both sides.

This book also *isn't* about getting a product to market or operations or how to inspire people. There are plenty of other books on that. This book is about VCs and founders working together or apart to build or destroy businesses.

Throughout the book, Jerry's sections are prefaced with "Investor View" and Liz's with "Founder View." If you see a word in bold, you'll find its definition in the glossary in the back of the book. Let's start with how the different positions of founders and investors lead to divergent views.

• • •

INVESTOR VIEW: A SYSTEM BUILT ON TRUST

Right at the beginning of books about venture capital is where the paean to startups and Silicon Valley usually goes. I believe in the Silicon Valley–style venture capital system—it's behind the majority of the most innovative companies of the last fifty years—but if you want to read about that, pick up literally any other book on venture capital. I want to focus here on the one improbably important thing that makes it all possible: trust.

Every day, people I have never met, and usually never heard of, email me and ask me for money. I read all these emails, take them seriously, and sometimes, after a few weeks of work, decide to write them a check. On the face of it, this sounds insane and, in some ways, it is. I'll lie awake at night, wondering what the hell I'm doing. Why should I believe I can give a complete stranger money, based primarily on a mostly unverifiable story they are telling me, and hope that I would ever see *any* of it again, much less make money doing it? The intricate sequence of events that has to happen between me writing a check and someday getting a bigger check back is unlikely, to say the least.

You probably also get emails (check your spam folder) promising you vast amounts of money if you just spend a little bit of money up front. You know these are scams; what makes the emails I get different?

The difference is the aforementioned Silicon Valley–style venture capital system. Liz likes to say it's a construct. It's a system people built over time to make giving money to strangers more appealing. It is based on an understanding shared between founders and investors about how market value is created, what constitutes progress along those value creation paths, how that progress is measured, and what it's worth along the way. It depends on a community of investors who share information, trust each other's opinions, and can roughly predict how the other will act. It depends on founders believing in making founding their profession (at least for a little while), finding other founders to mentor them, and being willing to take a big risk—not the risk of starting a company, that's an ordinary risk, but the risk of partnering with someone who will give them money but demand shared control of their startup.

And last, it depends, and mainly so, on founders and investors believing that the other will follow these norms even when times are tough or there's easy money to be made by ditching them. It depends on a certain kind of trust: not necessarily personal trust, but trust that founders and investors will each follow the rules, through good times and bad.

The system doesn't always work. Every year some venture capital–backed company turns out to be a fraud. But, despite hindsight-looking bystanders exclaiming that giving money to strangers is doomed to fail, these frauds are rare enough or small enough that the system overall still makes sense. It's the more run-of-the-mill failures, the ones that rarely hit the media and are ambiguously described when they do, that threaten the system. These failures happen when things are not going perfectly—and they only rarely do—and either the founder or investor decides to bend the rules in their favor.

The rules of the system constrain both founders and investors. Each of them agrees to these constraints for different reasons. For investors, it's primarily about the money, but it's more than that. The rules stop the VC from maximizing their returns at the expense of the founder and other VCs, for instance. This is not a legal constraint, it's just how the system operates. A VC who ignores this rule will find they are not welcome in future deals. Other areas of investing don't have these sorts of rules. VCs accept these constraints because they believe they are doing something more worthwhile than other investors: They are promoting human progress.

Founders, also, agree to the system for more than money. They need money, of course, but for them money is a means, not an end. Just like you don't go to the hardware store to buy a tool, you go to get what you need to finish a project, founders don't go to VCs for money, they go for help realizing their vision of building a company.

The system promises both founder and investor that they can be successful while getting what they want. It does this by making money the medium: Investors have money, founders need money. And it rationalizes their different goals—self-realization and promoting progress—by denominating success in money. This is fine when everything is going well. But when things aren't going well, the symmetry breaks. When their goals and the path to riches start to diverge, founders may care more about their vision than making as much money as possible. Meanwhile, investors may decide that promoting progress is less important to them, in the end, than maximizing their returns. When this happens, when the founder and investor goals are no longer aligned because their definitions of success no longer agree, the system starts to break down.

FOUNDER VIEW: MY BET IS ON ME

There are two kinds of startups: those that take venture capital and those that are bootstrapped. The latter is like my first business or my stepmother's catering company or even a bed-and-breakfast financed with a bank loan. The venture-backed company is different. In today's world, it's someone buying a piece of your company for millions of dollars in the hopes that you can get your idea to be so big that it takes over or creates a market unto itself. It's the 1,000x return vs. the "just enough to survive" of my grandparents' generation.

HOW I STUMBLED INTO STARTUPS

My first company was an eBay-based consignment business way back in 2000. Why should someone give me their clothes instead of bringing them into a resale shop? I suspected that people who could afford nice things might also not want to go through the effort of running yet another errand and that these same folks were also annoyed that sometimes sales took a long time. I decided to offer item pickup, and also thought that eBay's platform would accelerate the sales process. Marketing consisted of me printing out flyers and placing them by hand on cars parked in well-to-do suburban areas. Two years later, I had built the company up enough that it supported me part-time in college and while looking for full-time work post-graduation.

I haven't started a business this way since. My first salaried role after college was as an account manager for a venture-backed adtech startup. My job was to figure out how many ads we had served, put those numbers into spreadsheets, and send them to the customer. I also answered emails. We were trying to sell a product to CMOs at really big companies without actually knowing what it was that we were selling, how to price it, or what the outcome was going to be. We were figuring everything out along the way. Somehow to me that just seemed normal, that every job was like this, but in hindsight I think my mind was blown.

Since then, I've been Co-Founder & CEO of two startups, worked for two others as an individual contributor, and spoken to countless founders and VCs.

The first time investors wired one of my companies millions of dollars, I shook uncontrollably. It was some combination of happiness and incredulity and fear. Deep-seated, irrational, totally rational fear. It took a few minutes for the shaking to stop. It happens every time I close a round of funding. To this day, I'm scared of what I've gotten myself into and I'm scared of the expectations and I'm scared of how much work it's going to be and I'm scared of the people I took money from and I'm scared that we (always with co-founders) won't be able to figure it out and I'm scared I won't learn fast enough and I'm scared I won't be enough and I'm scared of what I don't know.

I'm also enthralled. I'm about to embark on the new hardest thing I've ever done and *the money is on me*. *I'm* the bet. Every part of my body and mind is alive, vibrating. It's a fantastic high each and every time it happens (nine and counting).

I used to be most fearful that my team wouldn't be able to figure out the successful way forward, but having trodden that path a few times now, I know we'll get there. What I now dread most is the people I'm in business with.

I've learned the hard way that venture capitalists are beholden to one thing and one thing only: returns. They care more about money than my company's mission or the people who work there, and that includes me. There is no such thing as right and wrong for them. There is no such thing as character. There are only returns. I typically find that I'm under a microscope whether the company is doing well or not. My investors, my Board, will bear down hard in times of plenty and even harder in times of strife. They'll suddenly shift from being an investor to trying to control the outcome. But they've invested in someone they can't control. I am unemployable for a variety of reasons and this unemployability is *the* reason I became a founder. My bet is on myself. My investor's bet is on me. And yet the moment there's a blip, suddenly this person whose job *isn't* to run a company tries to control it, me, and the outcome.

I suppose one could argue that predictability is fantastic. If you know how someone will behave, then you can game out each play. But how am I supposed to do my job (building a giant company) if I'm also simultaneously doing another job (managing people I can't trust)? And then the obvious question: Why on earth have I taken venture capital? Why will I most likely choose it in the future if I'm to build something in software or hardware or climate or space or essentially anything that *isn't* a dry cleaning business?

INVESTOR VIEW: TRUST IS SO EASY TO LOSE

The venture capital system sets an implicit expectation that founders and investors are working toward the same thing: a successful company. This norm is enforced through stories of heroic founders and what they have built. These archetypes, though—and this is understood—are exceptions; they are the few who won the game, and the story also says that most won't. These stories polish out the flaws of everyone involved, as with all stories of heroes.

The misunderstandings arise when founders or investors discover the other does not act the same when things are going perfectly as when they are not. The shared vision of building a company in harmony goes out the window when the company strays from the path of value creation the system laid out. Founders decide to manage risk by slowing down instead of barreling ahead; investors decide to take a low-odds chance at a big win instead of prudently taking money off the table. The result is a loss of trust, and this leads to a breakdown of the system, both in this instance, and more broadly.

Remember, the construct is based on trust: the trust that venture capital is the best way to fund fast-growing startups in quickly changing and uncertain markets. When it works, the results are incredible. But when the founder and investor stop trusting the system, something has to break. It could be the founder, who gets fired, or the investor, who loses their reputation. But it's almost always the company. And when it's the company that is hurt, neither founder nor investor get what they want.

By the way, you're only a few pages in and you can already see that Liz and I don't always agree. Who should you believe? We're not asking you to believe; we want you to see that we have different points of view. How the person on the other side of the table thinks is more important, practically, than what you believe.

FOUNDER VIEW: WHY I TAKE VENTURE CAPITAL

I choose this system because in order to win, a startup needs to go very, very fast. And capital of this magnitude and ease enables me to get an edge on the competition. There's no other reason. I make a deal with the devil because I think I can win, and I want to see my vision come to life in the biggest way possible.

So what do I do? How do I make such a raw deal work (well enough)? I try to manage that devil as best I can. I try to mitigate the risk of investor interference—on my mental health, on the company, on our future—such that it's annoying at worst. I try to set an example by being open and honest, often to a fault. I try to treat my investors the way I want to be treated. I hope for the best, expect the worst, and probably spend too much time gaming out how to keep my job. Success for me is a great company, a product that shines, a nice chunk of change, and enabling my employees to put food on their tables. Success for the investor is a nasty good return. Somewhere in the middle we may find our peace, and it always starts with understanding.

JOINT VIEW: EXPECT PROBLEMS BUT DON'T LET THEM STOP YOU

Maintaining trust in the system requires trusting the person you've partnered with. The founder needs to trust the investor, the investor needs to trust the founder. But why would they?

To trust someone, you need to have a good relationship with them, respect their decision-making process, and count on them to follow through with their commitments. Every stage of the startup process challenges all three. This book talks about fundraising, agreeing on terms of the partnership, co-managing the company through the board of directors, growing the company, and exiting. Each of these requires both working together and letting the other do their work. Each of them requires founders and investors doing what they say they are going to do. And each of them requires founders and investors to maintain a relationship through good times and bad. It also requires both sides to let go of the need to control the other. Each chapter will talk about when these things don't happen, and why.

These problems are entirely predictable, but the people who build companies tend to ignore them until they can't, then ascribe them to idiosyncratic failure. In fact, they aren't idiosyncratic; they happen so frequently that they should be considered the norm. We have received some pushback (mainly from venture capitalists) that because the system works well enough despite these endemic problems, talking about them will only scare away founders without any countervailing benefit. We don't believe that. We believe founders and investors can make the system work even with these problems, *if they can see the problems coming.*

To repurpose an old cliché, giving money to strangers is the worst system of funding innovation, except all the others that have been tried. We can make it better. We start by using another pillar of building trust: being open and honest. The venture capital system requires a willing suspension of disbelief. As a result, most books about startups talk about solutions rather than problems. We are going to openly debate the problems so that we have a real basis for solutions. If this helps future founders and investors have a clearer understanding of what they need from each other, and where they often fail when trying to provide it, we will have done what we set out to do.

KEY TAKEAWAYS

FOUNDER	INVESTOR
Venture capital is one way of funding a company and it comes with both advantages and strings.	A partnership between founders and investors can make the company as successful as possible.
Because investors and founders have different objectives, trust is hard to come by.	The partnership relies on trust and a shared mission.
The company is personal for founders and about returns for investors, setting up the inherent conflict.	When a founder or investor ignores this partnership, the other feels betrayed and the company is threatened.
A functional relationship requires trust, which is not a given, but at least we can try to understand our counterpart.	Trust requires understanding, and that is what this book sets out to provide.

2

FUNDRAISING

INVESTOR VIEW: THE BEST AND WORST PART OF INVESTING

The first time I meet most founders is when they decide to raise money. They've come up with an idea for a company and maybe they've even built a prototype and hired a person or two. They've realized it might take some time before they can bring in enough revenue to cover their expenses, and they're looking for some money to cover that cost. That's what I and other venture capitalists do. We give founders money so they can build their businesses into something big. In exchange, we get a piece of the business and some say in how it's run.

I love parts of the fundraising process and hate others. I love meeting entrepreneurs, hearing their ideas, and having a conversation about what the future will look like. I learn new things, have to think hard about their consequences, and maybe get to help somebody start down the path of realizing their dreams. Other parts I don't love: I have to say no to most founders and deal with their disappointment (or even anger.) Even if I say yes, I'm still across the table from them, negotiating how much of their company my money buys and how much say I will get in how they run it. This is the stage where founders and investors first sense they might not entirely share the same definition of success. It's also the time that founders realize there's an information asymmetry between them and the VCs.

I've been involved in more than three hundred fundraising processes, sometimes as **lead**, sometimes as just someone who has to agree to the contracts. I know what's going to happen, what's reasonable, and what everyone around the table will say to things that people ask for. It's a big part of my job. It's a small part of a founder's job, or should be. A successful founder may only fundraise four or five times in their life. Good VCs know they can't screw the founder upfront: They have to work with them for years after they invest; it would be poisoning the well. But there's always some investor who tries to take advantage of founder naïveté and every founder has heard the stories, so while the VC is working to learn if they can trust this stranger who is asking them for money, the founder is working to see if this particular VC is one of the good ones or one of the bad ones. It's a rocky start to a potentially long relationship.

A MENAGERIE OF ROUNDS

VCs invest in startups a bit at a time. Each of these fundings is called a round. What each round is called drifts over time, but as of this writing the usual progression is this:

FRIENDS AND FAMILY

Exactly what it sounds like. The founder's friends and family give them a smallish amount of money—usually from $50,000 up to $250,000—to get started.

PRE-SEED

Funded by angel investors or small institutional funds, usually between $250,000 and $1 million.

SEED

Usually institutional funds specializing in Seed or a Seed program at a larger fund, who is using it to get to know companies before they raise real money. Between $1 million and $3 million.

SERIES A AND B

Primarily institutional funds. The Seed, A, and B rounds are often collectively called *early stage* though this moniker really refers to how far along the company being invested in is. Later stages are called *growth stage* because the money is being used to grow the company. These rounds vary widely in size, but A is often between $3 million and $25 million, while B can be as large as $50 million or more.

SERIES C AND LATER

Later rounds tend to get bigger, of course. But if a company gets to Series F or later, it means they have failed to find an exit and things may be getting tenuous.

• • •

None of this should be taken as gospel. The names and sizes here are just to give you context at the time this book was written.

FOUNDER VIEW: I LOVE FUNDRAISING

That's right. I FUCKING LOVE IT. It's the ultimate sale. How do you convince someone you don't really know and who doesn't really understand what you're talking about (sorry but not sorry at all, it's true) to wire a ton of money to the company bank account, solely on the strength of an idea? If it weren't for the fact that you actually intend on building a company, it would be the ultimate in con games.

Think about it: For founders, investors are typically only a means to an end, and that end is money to help me grow my business. We are united by the construct that is venture capital. At every fundraise, I marvel at the absurdity of it. Someone decided to buy a piece of the company for millions of dollars! The first time it happened, I took a picture of the bank account immediately after all wires had cleared, and I've done it every time since. At my last company, I'd do a live screenshare with the entire team every time we closed a round just to let the ludicrousness of it sink in. We'd all stare in silence. As your company gets larger, the smaller numbers lose their meaning (like the biweekly payroll approval will be larger than your Pre-Seed round) and so it takes more money to create the same level of shock, but it's always there.

It's also something that folks outside our world don't understand. Even my Uncle Lenny, who used to work as an executive for a storied American brand, said to me, "Lizzie, I just don't get it." The notion that someone will give you $5 million at a $25 million **post-money valuation** on $10,000 in **MRR** is absurd. The notion that this money comes from meeting someone three times is absurd. It's beyond absurd. It's actually pure insanity. It's based on people and an ability to perceive the future and an ability to believe in someone's view of the future and nothing more. And yet this is the paper-thin world we play in. It's fantastic.

So many founders tremble at the exercise. It takes too long or they can't get any traction or "nobody gets it" or the VCs want so many different things. They feel powerless, with no control over any part. They feel beholden to these money overlords and their purported wisdom. And then there's the term sheet and the docs themselves, and those are written in a foreign language.

Nothing could be further from the truth. The reality is that it's a game. Founders don't know enough to embrace it as such, and investors certainly aren't going to cede an inch of the purported power. This power dynamic is present in all stages of a company, but nowhere nearly as much as while fundraising.

I used to feel this way too, but slowly, slowly, I realized that this power dynamic was entirely within my control to change. I could overcome my overwhelming fear of docs, for example, with time, research, and self-education.

This fear makes sense, of course. Investors have done thousands of these in their career, perhaps tens of thousands at veteran funds, and VCs earlier in their career can tap more experienced partners at their firm. This is the crux of the problem: Founders do one, maybe two companies in their careers. VCs back so many more. As we'll see in the Terms chapter, the documents both groups sign have long-term consequences that to investors are the ABCs of their business, while founders are still just learning the vocabulary and find it intimidating. It's like buying a home without an inspection and then finding out in the 612th rainfall that the house was constructed exclusively with dead grasshoppers and your insurance doesn't cover that. You're now homeless, have thrown away hundreds of thousands of dollars, and you have no legal rights to try to get any of that back. That's being a founder.

INVESTOR VIEW: FINDING A NEEDLE IN A HAYSTACK

Despite hundreds of venture firms doing thousands of deals a year, a new founder's first fundraising problem is getting just one of them to pay attention. VCs are not hard to find; they have to deploy large sums of other people's money into startups over a short period of time, so they are always on the lookout for good startups. It's their job. What VCs are selling, and what founders are buying with a piece of their business, is a commodity: money. Buying money is like buying bottled water: You may decide to pick this bottle over that bottle because of price or brand or form factor, or just because it's what's available, but what's in the bottle is always the same: water. The venture capitalist is the bottle; they're just a snazzy vehicle for the money. If you're headed out to explore the desert and someone offers you a Dasani, you don't sit around until a Fiji shows up.

Investors need to see many, many companies to make good investments, so they need to meet many founders. But how? If you're a VC trying to find founders, it's pretty hard. You can wander the halls of your local engineering school, but you'll mainly be buttonholed by professors who want you to pay them to do noncommercializable research. You can head to local entrepreneurship meetups, but you'll just meet a bunch of accountants and other people trying to sell services to small businesses, not people trying to start businesses. There is no good way to reliably find founders just as they are starting out.

Rather than try to find founders, VCs generally try to make themselves findable. They create ways to get founders to reach out to them. Social media, content marketing, speaking at conferences, and getting themselves talked about gets them noticed by founders. But this kind of self-marketing by VCs and VC firms is inexact. They can't tell founders what they are looking for, except in the broadest terms, because they're looking for something new (and if they knew exactly what that was, they'd be founders, not VCs). So they market themselves broadly and end up saying no to almost everyone who reaches out to them. If you're a founder, this sucks. It sucks for VCs too: If people only emailed me with deals I wanted to do, it would save me a shitload of time. But almost all venture firms do it this way because no one has found a better way.

If this is so, why do so many VCs make it impossible to get hold of them? Benchmark, for instance, is one of the top VCs in the world. They've invested in some companies you've probably heard of: Dropbox, Twitter, Uber, Snapchat, Instagram, Discord, Domo, New Relic, Nextdoor, WeWork, Yelp, Zendesk, Zillow, and so on. A founder might be excited to show them their business idea. They go look at Benchmark's website, but there's nothing there: no description of what they do, no email address, no telephone number, no list of partners, no list of companies. There are a couple of physical addresses, but they are not suggesting that you snail-mail them a pitch deck nor just drop on by (though I'm sure plenty of people have done both). The only reason they have the address on the site is so people they've invited to the office don't have to keep calling and asking where it is. If they really want to be pitched, why don't they make it easier?

Benchmark is like an elite club: You don't reach out to them; either someone they know recommends you or they reach out to you. They only stand out because their website is so obtuse. Most VCs have some content on their websites, and some even have emails to send unsolicited pitches to. But it's still hard to get their attention, and this isn't just a flaming hoop they've put up for founders to jump through for their amusement (maybe a bit, idk). They make themselves hard to get to because very few VC firms are set up to deal with the fire hose of pitches they would get if they made themselves available to all.

SET BOUNDARIES

When I was young and stupid, I accepted an invitation to speak at the biggest tech trade show in the world, held in Las Vegas. I got on a stage with a couple of other panelists and answered questions in front of a crowd of hundreds of tech folk. After the panel, my fellow panelists fled out the back of the stage. I stayed to talk to people. "Here's my chance to meet some awesome potential founders," I thought. A long line formed, and I talked to people and handed out business cards. I must have handed out two hundred cards. When I got back to the office, the business plans rolled in . . . scores of them. I read them all. It took a long time. They all sucked.

I'm not Benchmark, but even I get besieged with pitches. If I tell people I invest in startups, about one in twenty wants to either tell me their idea or introduce me to someone they know who has a startup: a nephew, the daughter of a friend, a co-worker, a friend from school, or any of a hundred other tenuous connections. This leads me to believe that at least 1% of the US population has a plan they would like someone to give them money to pursue (erring on the low side because I don't know how representative my sample is). That's three million would-be startups. On the other hand, there are only a few hundred companies that go public every year, on average. This suggests that the vast majority of those millions of startups are not VC fundable.

The job of the VC is to get from the millions to the hundreds. Finding a company to invest in is an exercise in weeding out, as quickly as possible, the ones you *won't* invest in. Making yourself hard to find is partly just a defense against having millions of plans show up in your inbox and partly a way of immediately disqualifying people who can't find a way to end up in it anyway.

This seems to conflict with actually doing the job: investing in startups. *Some* of those millions of unfunded ideas must be good ones. Why would I, and Benchmark, not look at them? If we could look at all of them and just find the best ones, we would probably do better (and certainly no worse) than by not looking at them.

The problem is, we can't look at all of them. Looking at a company is a time-consuming process. I reserve Fridays for reading all the pitch emails in my inbox. Most Fridays I email back a "thanks, but no" to all of them. I'm pretty clear on my website and in my various online bios about what I invest in and what I don't, but many of the pitches I receive are not things I am qualified to evaluate. They are outside my area of expertise, or my geographical area, or need more money than I can invest, or, or, or. Investors do better when they invest in fairly specific things. That's why there are New York City–based Pre-Seed **SaaS** funds, for instance, or San Francisco growth-stage **direct-to-consumer** funds. When founders send a business plan to a random investor, chances are they don't fit the investor's **thesis**.

Not that my thesis is that precise. Like most investors, there is a tension between my not wanting to look at companies I can't evaluate and not wanting to miss that once-in-a-generation startup because it is slightly outside my thesis. The thesis has to be both narrow and broad. My favorite was NYC-based IA Ventures' "Big Data." This was both precise—your company should be driven by the progress in data storage, analysis, and use—and vague—everything uses data, and "big" is in the eye of the beholder.

The thesis also changes over time, and this can confuse founders. At one time I invested in several adtech startups, and people knew me for that. But after a few years I had both too much of my money in that one basket and felt like the space was getting crowded, so I stopped focusing on it. Now, even ten years later, I still get more than my share of adtech pitches.

Even the companies that fit my thesis, I won't meet most of them. I have to say no; there are too many of them. I have no choice but to filter, even though I don't have that much information because I haven't met with them. It's a bit of a catch-22. My first filter is how we were connected.

One way VCs connect to founders is to proactively reach out to the startups they like. This only works, though, if the company has done something noteworthy or if the VC knows the founder from some other context, like a previous company.

Calling after the startup does something noteworthy is an option, but tricky: You won't know about them until they make some noise, but you also don't want to be the thirtieth VC to randomly spam them. Some VC firms handle this by having associates who do nothing but keep track of companies in certain segments, hoping to be the first to hear about news. Liz is going to say not to talk to these people because they are not the decision-makers, but I disagree. They are not the decision-makers, true, but they are great sources of information, and when the time comes for the startup to raise money, having that relationship can get a founder in front of a decision-maker very quickly.

The VC firms that do this kind of outreach are later-stage firms, and they are looking for later-stage companies. But VCs also do outreach to new startups, in a way. They keep in touch with people who are the likeliest to start new companies: people who have previously founded a company and are still hungry, and early employees of startups that have become very successful. The latter are people who have seen how it is done, so aren't intimidated to try it themselves.

I do the same. I keep in touch with people likely to start companies, and even encourage them. And, of course, I keep in touch with people I have backed before who have **exited** their companies. We talk about ideas and possibilities, and if they decide to go for it, I sometimes write the first check. I always introduce them and vouch for them to other VCs. But I can't reach out to people who I don't know are starting companies. I need them to reach out to me.

Of these, I pay most attention to the qualified pitches, the ones someone else has recommended to me. The people recommending them are usually other founders, who know what it takes to build a company, or other VCs. I trust that these people won't send me really bad ideas (and if they do regularly send bad ideas, after a while I stop paying attention to them). This is usually the first filter: Do I trust the judgment of the person who introduced me to the startup?

This has a big downside though: It means you can only invest in people in or adjacent to your network, and that ends up excluding a lot of good people. Being innovative, after all, is about doing things no one else is doing, and a big part of that comes from the people who do them; people who aren't exactly like all the other business executives are more likely to think differently.

THE TRUTH ABOUT BIAS

This is especially acute if everyone you know is pretty much exactly like you. Many VCs are either too lazy or unable to expand their networks, and that's why startup founders are overwhelmingly similar to VCs: white male Ivy League graduates.

VCs think they are mitigating their risk by investing only in the devil they know, even though they would increase their returns by finding the best possible founders, whether they are in-network or not. Besides being a bad investment strategy, since it excludes deals that could be blockbusters, it's also ethically wrong.

Just to be clear: I'm not exempting myself from this criticism. And I'm not saying that every VC is a sexist, racist, or elitist. This is a classic example of systemic bias, where past overt bias has caused the conditions for its own perpetuation. Only actively trying to change it will make any difference.

When founders reach out, I want to know they're reaching out to me specifically. When a cold email is obviously sent to a whole list of people, I don't feel very special. And I want to be special, because I don't want to be competing with hundreds of other random investors to give you money; that's a sucker's game. The standout founders are the ones who let me know they are reaching out to me because they think I can offer more than just money. I may just be a water bottle, but I'm the right water bottle for them.

A founder never really knows if a particular VC is going to be interested and whether they are looking to make an investment at that particular time. Sometimes a VC just woke up on the wrong side of the bed that morning and thinks every pitch they see is bad. Smart founders will pitch multiple potential investors. That means that if I got the introduction, several other qualified investors got it too. If the founder is impressive and has a good idea, I don't have long to make up my mind. I have to quickly figure out if the founder (and team) are who they say they are. And the only way to do it quickly is to start before everyone else. There are three ways to do this: Reach out to them, as discussed; be among the first people the founder thinks to contact; or pay attention to good founders who have pitched an uninteresting idea . . . if you can help them develop a better idea, you will be the first to know about it.

Founders will talk to any investor who will listen, and that's just good sense. But the first ones they try to talk to are the ones who have a reputation for being helpful. If they think you can help them refine the idea, and perhaps introduce them to other investors, they will reach out to you early in the process. For this, you have to be the kind of person who helps, but founders also have to *know* you're that kind of person.

The best way is when other founders recommend you. For this, be straightforward and helpful to founders you invest in; that's table stakes. But also, be straightforward and helpful to the founders you *don't* invest in. That makes a real difference, for two reasons. First, you won't invest in most of the founders you meet. Either they'll pitch you and you have to say no, or you won't even get that far with them. If you can be helpful to some of the few founders who you invest in, that's great. If you can be helpful to the much greater number of founders who you don't invest in, that's just a lot more people out there singing your praises. And second, if you helped them just because it's the right thing to do, it tells them you might be more than just the greedy bastard they assumed you were.

Second best is when founders read about you and decide you're the right investor to contact. Every VC is writing or tweeting or on podcasts or speaking at events. If you want to stand out, try to actually write or say something both true and useful. Stop recycling the same old entrepreneurship clichés. Noobs might be impressed if your big value-added message is that they should "talk to customers" or "iterate, iterate, iterate," but once any founder thinks about it for a second, they will realize this is the mindless advice they could have gotten for free pretty much anywhere. Being thoughtful makes you different.

But better than both, for a lot of reasons, is when you meet an inspiring founder before their idea is fully baked. If you think they can evolve their idea from not great to extremely viable, and you can help them do that, you get several benefits. You get the satisfaction of actually doing something innovative, you get to know how the founder thinks and works over a period of time, and you earn their trust. Not least, you get the first look at what they are doing.

FOUNDER VIEW: HOW TO CUT THROUGH THE NOISE

Yes, there is certainly no shortage of venture capitalists, with more popping up daily. There are real investors, investors that claim they're investors but are really just moonlighting to feel cool or don't have enough money, investors who say they do Seed but really do Series F, **corporate arms, PE funds**, your mom and dad and cousin and friend you sat next to in college chemistry class who has a small fund . . . they're literally everywhere. I used to go to San Francisco so frequently for work that I started dating there. It was a joke at first and then it became plain sad: Everybody I went out with, when they heard what I did, talked about their fund and asked me whether I'd take their money. There was the investment banker, a chief strategy officer of a unicorn, and the roommate of a friend who let me crash on their couch. Everyone claims to invest, but you need to search to find the ones that can actually write you a check.

And then once you do, you can't raise money from them unless they're willing to talk to you. And as a first-time founder, you most likely don't have a network of investors you can call on, which means it's actually really hard to get investor attention. It's daunting to even think about creating that network. The later you are in your startup career, and especially if you've started more than one company, the easier it is to get folks to pay attention. But the first time is always the hardest.

WHAT IT TAKES TO FUNDRAISE, IN PLAIN ENGLISH

If you think about the chain of events that has to happen to get someone to give you some money for a piece of your company, it's nuts that we even try to do it: You have to figure out who to call and then you have to figure out how to get in touch with them and then you have to figure out how to get their attention and then you somehow need to say enough of the right words in a cogent-enough manner (impossible at this stage) such that they agree to a second and third call, and then you need to convince the rest of their team of everything you already told them and then you need to go through this thing called negotiating, with words you've never seen in your life, paying lawyers more money than your grandparents probably made in a year, and then you have to figure out how to get this round to close and then you stare at the money in the bank account and have to figure out exactly what the hell you do with it because everything in the past three months you made up anyway just to get the money.

A successful fundraise requires relationships, hustling, and audacity. Fear and anxiety have no place here. No wonder it's daunting.

For most second-time founders or beyond, getting in front of investors should be fairly simple, so I'm going to focus solely on the first company experience.

When I raised my very first round, it was 2010. I had just left a startup backed by two well-known funds. The founder of that company was both a friend and someone who was very well known for previously starting an early infamous messaging service. I was personally well known to other startup founders in the adtech space. I had a reputation as someone smart and bold. And yet I could barely get anyone institutional to pay attention when I tried to raise money. It was so hard, in fact, that my co-founder and I gave up after three months and instead raised $250,000 from angels. By angels, I mean my uncle and my co-founder's parents and incredibly generous people we had worked with previously. One of our employees even wrote a check!

That money enabled us to build enough product to raise a Series A in 2012 (no joke—$1.5 million—that's how much fundraising amounts have shifted compared to today's $20 million Series A). You'd think that would have been easier at that point, but nope, it wasn't. Even with industry names and national brand customers, even with friends in high places, it took us nine months to raise the $1.5 million from institutional funds. *Nine months*. Even with the connections we had, we simply didn't know (enough of) the right people to be able to run a fast, easy process, nor did anyone tell us that's what it would take. The angel round was at least large enough that funds were willing to pay attention the second time around, but we didn't have the cachet to move the fundraise quickly.

Fast forward: My second company took under a month to raise its $1 million Pre-Seed round. And whatever my third company ends up being, I'm already oversubscribed and that's without a technical co-founder, without an idea, and with a valuation that I'll probably ask to be marked down because I'll have fallen over my ski tips before I've even signed the incorporation documents.

It's really, really hard to get VCs to pay attention to you as a first-time founder, let alone serious attention. They receive thousands of unsolicited pitches and decks and emails every year. While they claim otherwise, this is why they employ associates: to do the drudge work. You have to find a way to cut through the noise. You must be charming, develop a relationship, and drive the process forward, while also coming to terms with your own gut as to whether or not you want to take their money. You have to do this without ever having done this before in your life. It's hard. And the plethora of funds today makes it even harder. I think about the potato chip aisle in a grocery store. VCs will see all the potato chips and get to choose which bag they want. You have to sit patiently on the shelf, worrying if you're eye level and if your bag is shiny enough and if the font is readable and whether or not the investor is worrying about their weight today or on a salt binge and perhaps today is the day that the entire world decides cinnamon and ginger are over as flavors and defaults back to plain old sour cream and onion. If Jerry's money is a commodity, then an investment in my company is based on the whims of the day. It's so hard that it's no wonder why some would-be founders never start.

First, you have to create a list of investors that are appropriate for your stage. How do you do it? **Crunchbase** may be some of the best money I've ever spent. It's a database of, theoretically, every round of funding with the ability to sort and filter and tag. It can be weird to use—like most software, it's a janky UI sitting atop a database, so if you don't get the vagaries of SQL, you'll miss things—but it does the trick.

You find a list of every fund that writes checks for your stage and industry. If you're a dating app, it's a waste to call on folks that primarily do **B2B** SaaS. Are exceptions made? Absolutely. Will they get made for you? No. The exceptions are done because they have a prior relationship with the founder or the install base is so good that the investor would lose their job if they didn't fund it.

Another secret is to home in on funds that are *actually writing checks*. One investment a year does not a Seed fund make. I found out the hard way that one **Tier 1** fund lets their partners write only two checks a year. We didn't know that (neither did any of our current investors, and that was even more of a surprise). It was September when we were raising, and it turned out that the **partner** had already made their two investments. Now, arguing on the flip side, if our deal had been interesting enough, they would have found a way to get it done, so perhaps this is one of those "investors never speak truth" situations. Either way, if you're Pre-Seed or Seed, look for funds that do tens of investments a year. If you don't see that many entries in Crunchbase, move on.

Later-stage is easier. Because you've raised at least one round before, or you've started a company previously, or because you're starting to sell, word is out. Another thing that associates do at later-stage funds is keep track of what is being funded earlier. Net: You're already on the list.

The best way of getting in front of an investor is getting an introduction. Founder intros from within the portfolio are the best, especially if they're from companies doing well. Investor introductions are fine, but only in the case of a Seed fund that doesn't lead later rounds.

There is another hack my last company used to great success once we had some customers. Investors, whether the intro is warm or you're reaching out cold, want to quickly figure out if you're worth their time. We hired someone to reverse engineer which investors funded each of our customers. In the email, we'd end by saying, "To get the inside scoop, you can reach out to [customers x, y, and z] within your own portfolio." And reach out they did. It's one of the best tricks in the book.

INVESTOR VIEW: WINNOWING AND DUE DILIGENCE

Once the investor has connected with a founder, they have to start figuring out whether they want to invest. For me, this is a process of listening, doing research, thinking through scenarios, stress testing the founder, and figuring out if this particular startup is the best place to invest my limited resources, both money and time.

Unless I already know the founder, the process usually starts with an email introduction with a two- or three-paragraph overview of their idea and themselves. As mentioned, I immediately weed out the kinds of things I don't invest in.

I email back those who survive the first culling and ask for a pitch deck or more information. I use this information to try to distinguish between obviously bad ideas and potentially not bad ideas. This is imprecise, though often not that hard. At least half the ideas I see are (metaphorically) some variant on: selling dollar bills for 90 cents; turning lead into gold, not realizing this would make gold worthless; a problem no one has solved yet because it's not worth solving; or, an idea I have seen tried a dozen times and fail each time.

SOME IDEAS ARE TOO BAD TO DIE

An idea I first saw in 1998, and have seen funded at least a dozen times since, is technology that can make clothing items in online video clickable. If you click on a character's awesome sweater, it will link to a store where you can buy that exact sweater.

Every time someone pitches this idea to me, I ask them why all the companies that tried it in the past have failed. They invariably have never heard of any of those companies; when startups fail early, they disappear without a trace.

This is an exciting pitch and I still have no idea why it's such a bad idea. But unless a founder can explain how they are going to avoid whatever killed all their predecessors, I am not going to invest in it.

Often, when I email asking to see the deck, the founder will instead ask to pitch it live, without giving me a chance to see it first. They want to control the narrative. Unless the founder has credible work experience or the introduction was from someone I really respect, I won't agree. At this stage I am going to say no to most pitches because even if it's not an obviously bad idea, it's usually an idea I'm just not excited by. If I have a choice between spending the next ten years working with a company that's doing something really, really interesting and where I might make a good return, and working with a company that's doing something I find boring but might make a good return, I'm going to choose the former. I can afford to be picky and I want to enjoy my job. So if I'm going to say no for idiosyncratic reasons, then no pitch, live or not, is going to change my mind. Why waste the founder's time, or my own?

I should note that not every investor is like me. Many, especially earlier in their career, want to see every pitch from a credible founder they can, even if they know for sure they won't be investing. They're using the founder to learn, even if this wastes the founder's time. Other VCs, of course, will look at anything they think can make them money.

If I think the pitch deck is interesting, I'll ask the founder to get on a phone or video call. In these calls I don't let the founder walk me through the deck; I have already read it. I use the pitch as a way to ask questions about things I didn't understand, didn't feel like I had enough information about, or didn't agree with. If the founder has a demo they can show me, that's even better. This all lets me understand what the founder is trying to do and also see how they respond in real time and off-script. I'll often have more questions after this call, and I'll email to follow up and ask them.

If I'm still excited, I'll ask the founder to meet in person. Not all VCs do this—especially when markets are frothy—but I have a hard time getting a feel for a person without talking to them face-to-face. This is especially important if there is more than one founder or if there is another crucial member of the team already on board. In those cases, I ask for the other party to come to the meeting too. I want to see how they work together.

After this initial winnowing, I start due diligence in earnest. I talk to potential customers about the problem the company is solving and other solutions they have tried (if they haven't tried other solutions, it must not really be a problem). I talk to technologists about feasibility and where the technologies being used are going. I think hard about where the market might go, who else might compete, and how others might react. I calculate how much money the startup will need, when they will need it, and how much someone might eventually buy the company for if they are successful. This is the bread and butter of VC work, and it's all relatively straightforward.

If I like what I find, I move on to the next stage: trying to figure out an offer that works for both of us. We'll talk about that more in the next chapter. I should note that other VCs like to have several meetings before they get here. Most notably, for VC funds, they have a partner meeting.

When a founder is connecting with a VC firm, they are, in fact, connecting with a specific partner. That partner will run the process to determine if they think their firm should invest in the startup. If they do, they will usually need to convince the other partners in the firm to agree. The end result of this is the partner meeting, where all the partners come together to hear the founder pitch. Different firms do this slightly differently, but the sponsoring partner guides the founder through it. If the partners agree, they will offer the founder a term sheet.

FOUNDER VIEW: PREMEDITATION IS KEY

It goes without saying that if you're going to try to fundraise, you should probably have a good idea. An idea doesn't need to be good in the sense that everyone gets it. In fact, when my last company pivoted early on and we introduced the idea to my co-author, he was dumbfounded that nobody else was doing it and it took a bit of convincing to show him otherwise. And Jerry's seen *everything.* In the end, it only matters that you can get *someone* to believe in it (although ideally more than one person). That someone, as Jerry mentioned, will be a partner.

When it comes time for you to raise, know that it's nothing more than a sale and your job is to raise as quickly as possible. You do that by creating FOMO. Investors want to take as much time as possible. They don't want their hand forced, and their job is to wait as long as possible to invest so as to minimize risk. The following strategy is designed to put power back into the founders' hands by playing the game *you* want to play, not the one they want you to.

Here are the stages of fundraising as I see it:

1. Map out the raise: who, when, how (covered in "Founder View: How to Cut through the Noise" earlier in this chapter).
2. Craft and test the narrative: story, objection handling, deck.
3. The raise itself: implementation of points 1 and 2.
4. Term sheet negotiation: the basis for the next ten years of your life.

5. Docs: these ten years, in a language you don't speak and need to become fluent in, in about a week.
6. Close: herding sheep and keeping your cool.

This chapter will cover the first three with the remainder covered in Terms.

Narrative

The second phase in a raise is to craft a story that sells. Most (read: all) founders put together a deck that follows a classic trajectory of lots of words, lots of slides, a **TAM** slide, **use of funds** (graphs that go up and to the right), competition. This is wrong. It's a nice framework that does cover the bases investors will eventually insist upon, but it distracts from the goal of crafting a story that sells. If you put words on a slide, investors will spend time reading instead of listening to you. If you put a competition slide in, it introduces objections into your narrative.

The narrative must strike fear into the heart of the investor, and then serve up your company as the solution to that terror. Then you introduce some indication that you have traction in some area, present the team as cohesive, and then tell them how much you want. That's it. Competition, market size, product demo—all this should be deferred until the second conversation. The narrative is designed to get you into a second call, and then a third, and then a partner meeting. Like any sales call, your job is to get to the next step, not to finish everything at once.

The opening slide to my last Series A raise was authored by one of my co-founders. It was a picture of someone standing outside on a rainy day, trying to hail a cab. The talk track was this: "Remember what it was like to stand in the rain and try to hail a cab? Then someone invented an app and it changed your life forever. That's the

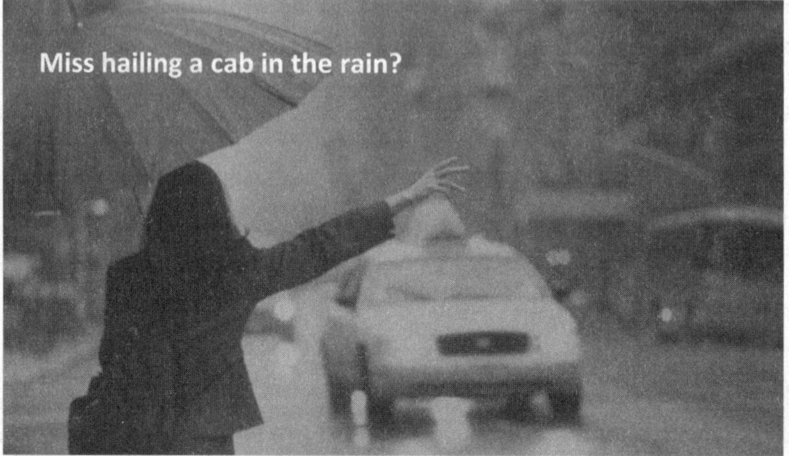
Miss hailing a cab in the rain?

feeling DevOps teams get when they see strongDM for the first time." Laugh-inducing? Yes. Did I turn to my co-founder and say, "You've got to be kidding me" when I saw it? Yes. Did he insist we were going to do it? Yes. Did it take me something like fifteen times delivering it before I could do it with a straight face? Yes. And was he right that it was utterly and totally effective at setting the stage and causing folks to laugh but, most important, laugh and be keyed in and getting it? Yes, he was.

If I had to craft a deck in words, irrespective of fundraise stage, it would be this:

1. The world is ending.
2. In the worst possible way it could end.
3. And whatever you think you know about preventing world explosion, you are wrong.
4. Meet The Best Company Ever!
5. We are your savior.
6. We are already on a rocket ship.
7. Here's how the founders look in PowerPoint bubbles, which gives you confidence to wire us money.

8. Here's the money we want.
9. Thank you.

Eschew the Fundraising 101 template and work on a narrative that puts *you* in control. You tell the story that communicates your vision, and use the framework *you* want, not the one that investors want you to use.

Take the TAM slide, for example. It's the slide that says, "This market is *so big* that if we even own 1% of it, we'll have crushed it and you'll have paid back the fund." Investors ask for it because (1) they need to see a large enough number such that they can validate to their investment team that the space is big enough to place a bet in, (2) they don't want to do that work themselves, and (3) they have to hear directly from the founders as to how they're going to own that number because they need to believe they're investing in founders who want to go all the way to **IPO** (more on this later). Founders create the slide because (1) the VCs ask for it, and (2) they have to practice saying falsehoods out loud so that they can get funded, because nobody will fund a company operating within a $40 million market. Without all this, the fable isn't complete.

Guess what else? The content of the slide itself is *pure fiction*! I have created at least five TAM slides in my career. They're built by calculating how many potential customers there are in the universe and backing into the total amount of money everyone will pay for your product. In B2B SaaS, you can build it bottoms up (users at a company) or top down (number of companies) and you should probably do it both ways so that the math vaguely works out if anyone questions it. And yet . . . the math itself is fiction. You need to know it cold in case you get asked questions about it, but it's one of those holding-the-finger-to-the-wind-type things.

Case in point: Imagine I have a company that sells birthday candles. This would be its TAM slide:

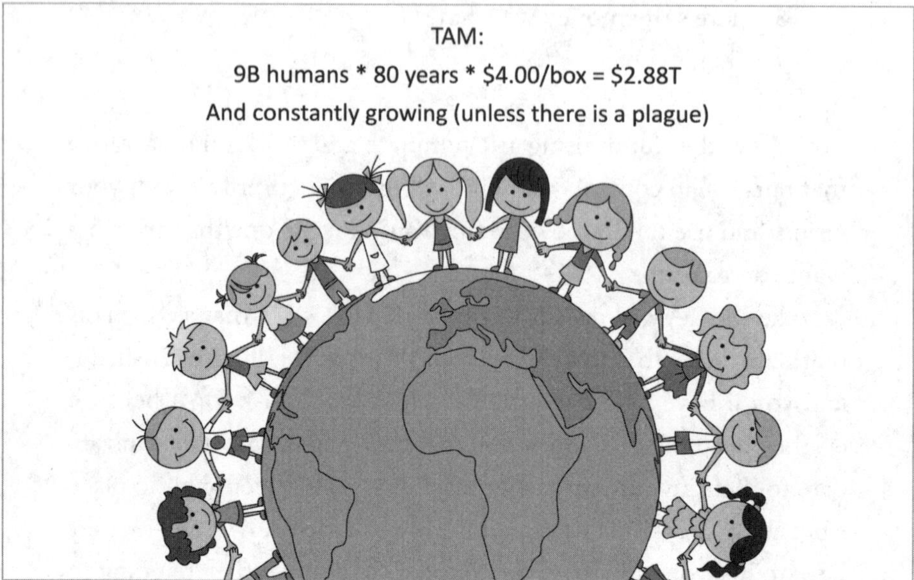

Image licensed by Ingram Image

Do you think if I presented this to any firm on earth they would actually believe I could capture $3 trillion in revenue, let alone 1% of it? If you think that, you should start a birthday candle startup right now. Imagine building this slide for a startup, say, selling a new database. Every company in the world has a database! It's lunacy, *but this is the math that's expected and bought into every day.*

When raising, it's also critical to be confident and perceptive enough to answer the question you want to answer vs. the one you're being asked. A good salesperson knows where they need to take their prospect and how to take them there.

For example, what if an investor asks, "But doesn't AWS already do it?"

1. **Parse what it means:** "I think the clouds have already won." This means the investor either already has a well-thought-out thesis or they're totally uninformed and throwing out words that make them sound smart.

2. **Identify what needs to be addressed in your response:** You need to reframe the problem so that the investor thinks about your company differently or gets educated on the real issue (not AWS).

3. **Answer the question you really want to answer:**

   "Infrastructure has changed. The cloud enabled companies to ingest more data because more data means better decisions. AWS created Redshift, a modern data warehouse, but it's expensive. Companies today can't capture, leverage, and use data in a cost-efficient way. AWS only solves capture; in order to help companies, you must solve all three, *and more cheaply*. Why? Because otherwise the cost of a modern-day business is prohibitive. That's why we win. Have you spoken to your portcos (portfolio companies) who are also our customers? Call them!"

4. **Outcome:** You've reframed the question to be about the actual problem and what a solution looks like. And you've redirected their attention to folks they trust that they will call the moment you hang up the phone. Game over.

The Raise Itself

To get a term sheet, you must get one to fall, and then everything falls into place. You'll either get more or everyone else will say no.

YOU JUST NEED ONE TO SAY YES

During one Pre-Seed fundraise, we were trying to get just one firm to say yes. It was down to the wire and tough going.

I got on the phone with the head of a well-known fund who was notorious for speaking his mind. I put the call on speakerphone so that I could type out what he said. My boyfriend at the time was standing next to me, cooking dinner. The investor was livid and accused me of bluffing in an attempt to get him to be the first to commit money (he was right). After fuming for a few minutes, he hung up on me but not before saying, "Well, if it's the difference between giving money to a woman or a cokehead, I'd rather give it to a woman. You have my money." My boyfriend turned to me and asked, "Why can't a woman be a cokehead?"

Twenty-four hours later, the entire round was committed (in spite of the paradoxical sexism). When one falls, they all fall.

The Fundraising 101 template here says to email a bunch of investors and pitch them all at once. I reject this. While you may have a narrative, you don't know how well it will hit. You don't know that it can't hit better. You don't have a sense of the first-, second-, and third-order objections that will arise. You don't know a lot. Fundraising is like trying to figure out exactly what product people will buy. It requires tons of testing. So before you pitch the firms you really want, you best be ready, and ready means iteration.

It's also critical to consider that in order to get term sheets to come in at the same time, they all have to be at the same stage in the process. The way to do this is by pitching in waves. Waves are designed to maximize your chance at success by pushing all of your learning up front. By the time you speak to "the best" investors, your story is airtight:

	Week 1	Week 2	Week 3	Week 4	Week 5	Week 6	Week 7
Practice	1st meeting	2nd meeting + diligence	Partner meetings				
Kind of Care		1st meeting	2nd meeting + diligence	Partner meetings			
Care			1st meeting	2nd meeting + diligence	Partner meetings		
Really Care				1st meeting	2nd meeting + diligence	Partner meetings	
Backups					1st meeting	2nd meeting + diligence	Partner meetings

* If you're doing this right, everything will start to coalesce in the shaded area

A co-founder and I developed this over a number of years, and believe me, it's *money*.

The first wave is practice funds. You don't care about them and you don't really want them on your **cap table**. It's the Tier 4s. They will ask all the standard questions and objections and will provide an outstanding base for the next wave. The second wave you sort of care about, the third you do care about, and then the fourth you really care about. Then there's the fifth: your backup funds, your safety net. You start a wave a week. You schedule partner meetings for each wave on the same Monday, and if you need to accelerate future waves because you're having so much success with the current one, you do that. (Note: Silicon Valley partner meetings are held Monday mornings. If you are invited to a meeting on a Monday morning and it's not labeled, it's a partner meeting.)

Now, when you go out, you are out. There is no starting slowly. Word gets around. Investors are the biggest gossips in the universe. Seriously—associates do this for a living. Their job is to get in bed (often literally) with other associates in order to get a sense of where deals are. They are incestuous in figuring out where a deal is, and then once they've decided to do a deal, they are mortal enemies.

Folks will also say to start fundraising when you have no fewer than nine months of cash in the bank. It's designed to ensure your back isn't against the wall. While I hear that perspective, timing is *everything*. I'd hold off on raising until you have enough of something to be able to create interest. Without it, you're dead in the water anyway and then you've wasted three months raising instead of focusing on the business.

Remember—investors want to defer saying yes for as long as possible. By architecting the raise like this, you maximize your ability to have all the landmines identified before you talk to the funds you really care about, and you also maximize your ability to have the raise go quickly. If you get one partner meeting set up, the other funds will scurry to do the same. They don't want to miss out. FOMO.

INVESTOR VIEW: PEOPLE, PRODUCTS, MARKETS

Founders are selling their vision, and this is what investors want, the bull case, the scenario where they make money. But sales pitches rarely give all the needed information. As an investor you will see dozens of companies a month. All will convincingly tell you they'll be the winner-take-all of whatever industry they are entering. You need to decide who is right, who is wrong, and who is just telling you a story. In some sense you have to know more than the founders about their business. But if you knew more than the people who are going to start and run the business, why would you give them money?

In venture capital you will always, in the end, not have all the data you need to make a rational decision. You have to take a leap of faith. Part of that leap is believing something you can't be sure of, no matter how much due diligence you do. It's a truism that if a founder is doing something no one has ever done before, you can't reliably predict what will happen.

UNKNOWN UNKNOWNS

Last year I asked a founder who had just started their company to come talk to my entrepreneurship class. They gave their pitch, and after they left, I asked the class, "What more do you need to know before you could decide whether to make an investment?" Students variously said they would need to see the product working, if customers would actually pay and how much, how much it would cost to acquire a customer, how quickly and well the founder could hire people, how long customers would stay as customers, how competitors would respond, and so on. These are all good questions and crucial to understanding whether the business is viable and how much it might be worth. I then tell them that none of that information will be available until after they invest, because the founder needs the money to finish the product, sign up customers, and pay salaries if they want to find the answers. "How many of you would invest, even if you can't know these things?" Very few raised their hands. I revealed that I had already invested in the business: It was definitely not a sure thing, but it was a good bet. The point I was trying to make was this: Every founder, the students in my class included, has to let go of certainty to get started. This lesson is contrary to all of their schooling to date, where certainty was rewarded with good grades. The startup world humbles the certain, and the more sure of yourself you are, the harder this lesson will be.

The founder narrative is usually primarily about why their company needs to exist in the world: what problem it solves and for whom; how enormous that problem is; and how, paradoxically, no one else has noticed this enormous market.

Your job as an investor is to try to glean some facts from this narrative. What is the entrepreneur telling you about the market, about their product, and about themselves and their team? You need to do this fast, because the sooner you can weed out companies you're not going to invest in, the more time you can spend learning about the rest. Make sure that in every conversation you are getting the information you need to go to the next step.

To make a decision when you have so little information and you know that even some of that information is not rock-solid, you eventually have to make a leap of faith. A guy I knew—super-smart, ex-McKinsey—was brought on as a partner at a major venture firm. After about a year he had still not made any investments. "There's something wrong with every company I see," he told me. Well, yes, same here. But if you don't write checks, you aren't a venture capitalist. (He eventually left the industry to be an executive at a large corporation, where he excelled.) I made this mistake when Liz pitched me on her last idea: It seemed too good to be true, so I questioned whether it was. It turned out she was right, but I can't take credit for being informed. I invested because of her, not the idea.

VCs look for three things: people, product, and market. Some say the people are the most important thing. Arthur Rock, the legendary venture capitalist and an early backer of Intel and Apple, among others, once said, "I invest in people, not ideas. . . . If you can find good people, if they're wrong about the product, they'll make a switch, so what good is it to understand the product that they're talking about in the first place?"

Some say the product, or idea, is the most important because without a great idea you have nothing, and the person who came up with the idea may or may not be the best person to turn it into a company. If it's truly a good idea, you can always find someone to monetize it.

All agree that the market has to be huge. Don Valentine, the founder of Sequoia Capital, said, "I like opportunities that are addressing markets so big that even the management team can't get in its way." But the best answer I've heard to the people/product/market question, though, is from Andy Weissman, a partner at Union Square Ventures. I once asked him which of the three he thought was most important. He said, "Why would I have to choose?"

Market

The market is the customers who are buying your product. It is also the total value of all the product you could possibly sell. And it is the totality of your competitors. When VCs ask about a founder's market, they're asking all these things.

When they ask who the customer is, they're asking something specific. They don't want to hear "millennials" or "people with smartphones" or—the very worst—"everyone." (Unless the startup is selling birthday candles, as Liz mentions, your market isn't *everyone*. We'll get to why birthday candles are a bad idea later.) Startups need to focus.

Who is the customer? "The customer is the chief security officer of a company that needs to pass a security audit." This is the kind of specificity that works best. Or, for a consumer-facing company, "Well-heeled smartphone users in their thirties and forties in dense urban areas." I always ask this exact question, and it's amazing to me how many founders stumble over it. They think they will launch a cool product and customers will just appear. "Build it and they will come." It almost never works this way.

I'm about to tell you the market you're going into needs to be really big. Then you're going to ask me which is it: a very specific customer base or a big market? It's both. I didn't say it was easy.

VCs make risky investments; that's what they're for. So most of a VC's investments fail. The rule of thumb is that one of the companies in their portfolio should "return the fund": Make all the money they invested in their entire portfolio back with a single company. They just don't know which one.

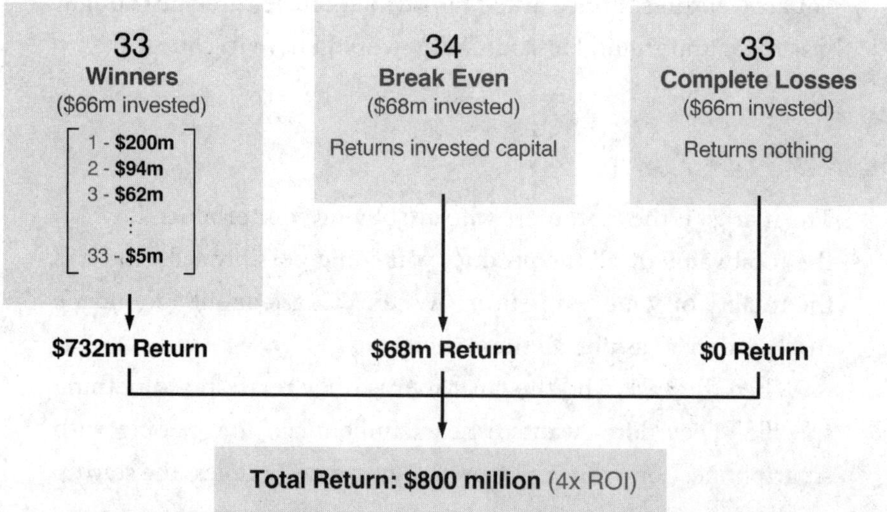

This chart depicts an imaginary early-stage venture fund. It invests $200 million in 100 companies, $2 million per company. Each $2 million buys them 20% of a company (20% is a typical ownership goal for a VC). For a single company to return the fund, the VC's stake in that company must be worth $200 million. Since the VC only owns 20%, the value of that one company must be one billion dollars. (Because $1 billion x 20% = $200 million.) And again, because the VC doesn't know which one of the companies they invest in will be worth a billion dollars, all the companies they invest in must have the potential to be worth that.

Finding one hundred companies that each have a shot at being worth $1 billion is a tall order. We'll talk more about the pressure to grow the company in the Growth chapter, but the point for now is that to be worth $1 billion, a company must be in a very big market.

When I say it has to be a big market, I mean there has to be enough money being spent by customers that if the startup someday has a reasonable percentage of it, that's a lot of revenue. Usually VCs ask founders to tell them how big the market is. Founders make some assumptions, calculate a market size, and then they and potential investors argue about it.

MARKET SIZING

Over the years I have seen several pitches for companies that wanted to sell information to VCs about the startup market. "How big is the market?" I would ask. "VC is a $350 billion market!" they would tell me, that being the amount of money VCs had under management. But that's not *their* market.

There were about one thousand VC firms in existence then, and even if all of them paid $100,000 per year for the startup's data—which is a stretch, since many of those VC firms were smaller—the startup would only have $100 million in revenue. This is not a $1 billion market.

Market size is not easy to calculate. It depends on variables the founder may not be able to know yet: how they can price their product; who, exactly, the customer is; and so on. Calculating a market size for an innovative product almost always involves guesswork. On top of this, the product itself may change the market size. Uber had more revenue in the first three months of 2022 than the entire

US taxi industry did in all of 2013. Uber and its rivals massively grew the market for taxi service.

In this sense, Liz is right that market size estimates are a fiction. But even fiction has value. Part of the value of a market size estimate to me, as an investor, is to see the assumptions the founder is making: How much do they think they can charge, and why? How many customers do they think they can get, and why? How do they think the market will change over time? And so on. I also like to see the calculation because I want to know if the founders are thinking big. If the entire market is only $100 million, say, and I estimate that the company might take 20% of that market, so their revenue could never be above $20 million, some founders say, "So what? That is plenty." It may be plenty for them, but it's not enough to drive the returns a VC needs.

Implicit in this last example is that no company takes its entire market. As of this writing, Apple's extremely successful iPhone has only about 50% of the global smartphone market. And keep in mind that the smartphone market is a subset of the cellphone market is a subset of the phone market is a subset of the communications market. You have to be careful when calculating market size that you assume an appropriate share of whatever market you have sized. The more specific the market, the larger the share you can assume, but no company has ever had 100% of a potential market (not least because there are always some potential customers who forgo buying the product at all).

This is the flaw in Liz's birthday candle example. While the total market may be as enormous as she calculated, no one company could take even a small fraction of it; there are too many competitors. And even if there weren't, as soon as some company started making money in that market, there would be. It's too easy to start a birthday candle company, there are no **moats**.

Product

Here are the obvious things VCs want to know about a startup's product: Do your customers want it, and is it possible to build? Many founders decide to build their product because they, themselves, want the product or they know someone who does. A market of one isn't enough. They need to talk to a bunch of other potential customers and see what they say.

Even better is asking some of those potential customers to become actual customers by paying for the product. In my due diligence I might ask people if they will pay for the product, and they will say they would, but I can't know if that's true. People are always saying they want something when they don't—online privacy, for instance—but when they're asked to pay for it, or even do fifteen minutes of work for it, they suddenly start to hem and haw. Paying for a product is proof they want it. As a bonus, the startup putting the product in the hands of customers is proof they can ship it, something that's just as important, and just as difficult to know ahead of time.

SHIPPING PRODUCT

Years ago I invested in a company with a genius founder. He showed me a live demo of the product when I first met him and I was impressed. I asked when he would start signing up customers, because it was clearly good enough for some people to use. He said, "Just as soon as we add a couple of crucial features. You don't get a second chance to make a good first impression." (Or something like that, I can't remember his exact words.) I put some money in, and he *never shipped the product*. Every time I asked, he told me a variation on the same thing: It's not perfect yet.

After a year, he raised some more money, though not from me. After another two years, he needed to raise money again, but no one would give it to him. Investors realized he would never let customers use the product because it would never be perfect. This wasn't my biggest monetary loss as an investor, but it was probably my most disappointing. The demo alone was a great product.

Founders can't prove customers will pay when they don't have a product ready yet, perhaps because they can't build one without raising some money to hire people first. In these cases, founders will tell you that customers will be willing to pay once the product is ready. There's no way to verify this, but there are signals. How much the customer is spending to solve the problem now, and how much it would cost to switch, are data points you can look at. This isn't as good as having paying customers, but it's a lot better than nothing.

Even if customers want and will pay for the product, the startup has to be able to build it. Founders have pitched me all sorts of products—perpetual motion machines, AIs that can beat the market, a better calendaring product—that can't be built. Other products can't be built yet, like fusion reactors and quantum computers. And some products can be built, but not by the people the startup has or can hire.

Other products aren't hard to build, they're just hard to connect to everything else. Data analysis products need to be fed with data. Payment apps need to be connected to the banking system. Marketplaces need to be connected to buyers and sellers. The product itself may be very simple to build, but the connections may be very hard. Founders often don't understand this when they pitch.

THE HARD THING ABOUT INTERCONNECTED PRODUCTS

I had the privilege of backing the first neobank, Simple. They built an online-only, branch-free bank that wasn't based on making money by charging their customers surprise fees. Building the product itself was not easy, exactly, but it was doable. Connecting it to the banking system was hard. Not just because the banking system was running on legacy hardware and software designed for your grandparents' passbook savings account. The pre-existing banks were also not keen on helping their future competition get started, especially if those new competitors were being encouraged by their VCs to grow faster by spending more than they made. They either couldn't care less about some tiny tech startup who wanted to interconnect or were actively antagonistic. The powerful and successful hate innovation, especially if it might innovate them out of power and success. It's always a mistake to think you're going to show up with your idea and they're going to embrace it. Simple eventually cracked this problem, but it added a year to the launch schedule.

But the overarching question a VC asks themselves when wondering about whether a product can be built is this: Can *this* product be built by *this* team?

People

Somebody once asked me what distinguishes a good entrepreneur. "Winning," I said. Good entrepreneurs aren't like this and aren't like that. Good entrepreneurs succeed. Success can happen in a million ways, and all the ethical ways are equally good. There's been a lot of academic work on what successful founders are *like*, and it is, in sum, inconclusive. But many people (and many investors, who should know better) still believe founders have to be young, or technical, or men, or just generally resemble previously successful founders in superficial ways. This is cargo-cult analysis, and it leads to bad decisions.

MORE TRUTH ABOUT BIAS IN VC

When my co-author started her first company I tried to help by introducing her to investors who might be interested in funding her. I ran into one of these investors at a conference. "What did you think?" I asked. He said, "She seems arrogant. We're going to pass."

This is a funny thing to say in the startup world. I mean, any founder who really believes they are the one person in the world who can face a huge and intractable problem and beat everyone else, including some of the biggest and smartest companies on earth, to build it into a $1 billion company in just a few years is either arrogant, naïve, delusional, or has a huge chip on their shoulder. Anyone who has invested in successful founders has invested in arrogant founders.

"Is she more arrogant than your male founders?" I asked. His face literally went bright red before he turned on his heel and walked away. So there I was, winning friends and influencing people. I called Liz. "I think he's a no."

I don't really care if the founder fits certain stereotypes. I care if they can deliver. Normally, when you are hiring someone, you look for people with some experience, people who have done the job before. This is the only foolproof way to determine competency. But many founders have never done the thing they say they're going to do. This is often because people who have good jobs don't often just quit them to do something crazy, like start a company. But it is also because the founders are doing something *no one* has ever done before.

Many VCs think they can judge people after a meeting or two; they have a "gut feeling" about them. I can't tell you how many times I've heard this. It's dumb and wrong. Dumb because you should only use gut feelings to make decisions as a last resort: when you have no time and no other options. Wrong because the research shows that VCs who say they invest from the gut get worse returns than those who have a more analytic approach. Instead of gut, you need to get to know the founder.

There are three important things I look for in a founder. The first is that they can change their mind (but not too easily). Startups need a vision to get going. They need to make decisions about what to build and for whom. But as they start putting product in front of customers, they quickly start to find out all the things they didn't know: whether the customer wants this product, whether they are solving an important problem, how the customers are solving the problem now, whether the customer will pay for it, and so on. Some things they learn will be pretty clear and some things will be ambiguous. Either way they should change the hypothesis the entrepreneur started with to some extent.

Sometimes a founder will be so in love with their vision they can't change their mind, no matter what the evidence shows. And sometimes they are so indecisive they change their mind every time there is the slightest shred of new information, driving their team crazy. They have to be able to walk the line between those extremes.

The second thing is that they can put up with hard times and not fold. Founders who take on the hard problems are more likely to have outsized success, so these are the kinds of things VCs fund. Sooner or later, every founder finds themself in a situation that seems hopeless, but they need to be the kind of person who can keep going. Bleak situations can turn around and deliver a lot of value. But once the founder gives up, it's over.

The third is that they can act: They aren't afraid to ship a product that's not 100% done, they can hire employees, they can delegate responsibilities, they can spend the money they raised from me. If they're scared to do these things because they're afraid to make a mistake or they're afraid they'll run out of money, they will never be able to succeed. They took a big risk starting their own company, but some founders raise money then decide it's too risky to spend it. It's the kiss of death.

Many startups have more than one founder. This is generally a good thing; no one can do everything, and if two people have complementary skills and find each other before you invest, that's one less thing you have to worry about. You have to worry only if that's not what is actually going on: Sometimes people start companies with friends and not everyone is going to pull their weight. Sometimes in a group of founders only a couple have the skills the company needs long term. The other founders might be there because they were present when the group came up with the idea and it seems wrong to exclude them later, because they had some skills that were needed for a while but aren't any longer, or just because the founders wanted fellow travelers and these were the only people they could convince. This isn't a problem for you to solve; the founders need to solve it themselves. And they need to solve it before you invest; it will only get worse.

On top of that, many founders have never run a business before. They certainly haven't run the business you are investing in. They might, in fact, be a technologist who has never managed more than a handful of people. They have never managed revenues and expenses, they have never raised money, and they have never talked to a customer. These things become their primary job if you invest, but you can't know if they can do it. Ask yourself if they can learn, if they are coachable.

And last, but perhaps most crucially, you don't really know *them* at all, and you are about to give them a very significant amount of money. Can you trust them? Will they use the money effectively? Will they do what's best for the business and all its shareholders, including you? Will they do the right thing if things go badly? And, the question so few ask: Will they do the right thing if things go really, really well?

Venture capital is about more than finding good ideas and good people. It's about somehow becoming comfortable with what you can't know. And in the end, this mainly comes down to becoming comfortable with the founder. If the idea is wrong (and almost all are, at the beginning) but the founder is the right person, they will course-correct and your investment might still be worth something. If the idea is amazing and the founder is the wrong person, you will lose everything you put in.

FOUNDER VIEW: FOLLOW YOUR OWN RULES AND YOU WILL WIN

Here are some guidelines that move a fundraise more quickly and eliminate objections. I call them Liz's Absolutes of Fundraising. You may call them LizAF:

LizAF

Liz's Absolutes of Fundraising

Rule #1: You are more powerful together as co-founders than with a hero CEO. Tag team each call. Someone pitches, someone observes and takes notes and chimes in when something isn't hitting. The story is a dance that the two or three of you create. I have never had stronger raises than when I did it with co-founders next to me. After each call, analyze what went well, what didn't, what resonated, what didn't. Edit and pitch again. Every call is an opportunity to test new and improved messaging. Even if you go out on a limb and it falls flat, who cares? You have another call in twenty minutes.

Rule #2: Fundraising is your new full-time job. You no longer have another job. If you're doing it right, there are six to eight calls each day. My thirty-ninth birthday fell in the middle of a raise. That day, my co-founder and I had already pitched eight firms and I had a dinner to go to that night hosted by a fund still in the mix. I sat outside Hudson Yards crying because all I wanted was to be home alone with a piece of birthday cake, not talking. That should be you: exhausted and on the verge of tears because you are pushing *that hard* to get a term sheet. Done right, this can be done in a month, possibly less. One round I did was twenty-eight days, from first pitch to term sheet signature. Another: four days flat, and twenty-three hours from first email to the term sheet we ended up signing. These are outstanding numbers and yet I think it is achievable for anyone to complete a solid raise in a month.

Rule #3: Never talk to associates. That's right, you heard me, and yes, I disagree with Jerry. You find a way to break down the door to a partner or you don't pitch the firm. Associates have no power. They can only say no, never yes. Only partners can say yes, and most often they have to get other partners to agree with them. Why would you talk to someone who is empowered only to reject you? You wouldn't. And if you can't hustle well enough to get directly to a partner, that should say something to you about your sales ability. You can do better.

Of course you'll say to me, "But, Liz, the associates are blocking me." Okay then, have them bring a partner to a meeting. While associates exist to help the firm separate the wheat from the chaff and help partners get educated on your space, your job as a founder is to give your company the best possible chance of getting an investment. You can't do that with associates. It's impossible to convince someone to give you money who can only say no. I will add that it can be hard to distinguish associates from partners at firms where everyone is a partner. Simply reverse engineer what companies they've actually been on the board of (director, not observer) by reading press releases or by looking at when they graduated business school, and you'll easily figure out who is who.

Rule #4: Never send a deck out over email. That's right, I said that, and yes, it's also in direct contrast to my co-author. A demo video is great, but nothing more than three sentences on your business in writing. It's the same reason as Rule #3. Why give someone the chance to say no? You, the founder, are a master storyteller. You can only control the narrative live. If someone won't spend fifteen minutes on the phone with you to hear your story, do you really want them on your cap table? I didn't think so. Nobody is too good for fifteen minutes.

Rule #5: Always pitch with a deck. You may be surprised that I advocate for one. I don't with most software sales, but I do with VCs. The deck, if crafted properly, helps you control the conversation. Against the wishes of one of my co-founders, I once insisted we fundraise without one. I thought we could "just have a conversation" about the business. Two meandering calls later that neither investor remembered, I said yes to the deck. I was wrong and I'll never do it another way again.

Rule #6: Never do anything without being on video (or in person). VCs like to take phone calls in their car. Don't let them. Politely reschedule the meeting, even if it means rescheduling after they've joined the call from their cell. They don't know your business, you don't have their undivided attention, the signal will drop, you can't read their faces. There are a billion reasons why this puts you at a disadvantage. Don't let it.

My co-founders and I figured out this rule during our last Series A raise. After a few calls in cars, we agreed that we would gently ask them to reschedule. The first time we put this one to the test was with a partner at a Tier 1 firm. This partner was a woman—and I call this out because I, too, am a woman, and often women are purposefully mean to other women. She joined the call on her cell while driving her car. We politely asked her to reschedule. She instead pulled her car over to the side of the road and got on Zoom, just to make a point. We had a rejection email something like an hour later. A few years later, she emailed again in pursuit of the company's Series B but her email went unanswered. Like all investors, she was as short on memory as founders are long.

Rule #7: Make your appearance a nonissue. Insomuch as our industry believes it's woke, it's not. Women are treated poorly, often by other women. The rich male investors are just as sleazy as you read about in the news, sometimes more so because they have no checks on their power. When in doubt, simply look the part you're playing. For example, if you're technical, dress like a stereotypical developer. Early on I made the mistake of wearing a suit and heels to a pitch and the VC probably still doesn't believe I was the company's backend developer.

In any case, looking dowdy is the best way to ensure the focus is on the business and not you. For women, and especially women who are attractive, I'd recommend knockaround clothes. Leggings, Doc Martens, sweatshirts, loose-fitting jeans, glasses instead of contacts. No fun colored hair. The goal is to blend in for male investors, and for female ones, you need to appear as nonthreatening as possible. For men, wear jeans and sneakers and a T-shirt, and I don't mean $500 kicks. You have to look like an engineer, not a Columbia MBA.

All co-founders need to be looked at, absorbed, and dismissed visually within the first five seconds. My co-author will most likely disagree with the entire previous paragraph, largely on the merits as it relates to presenting an idea that will make people money. I hold a more cynical view based on personal experience.

Rule #8: Investor data requests are dumb. The term is data room, and in this case I'm referring to information you use in the fundraise to convince investors to say yes and *not* what is required as part of diligence before closing. These data rooms exist simply because this is an investor wanting you to do their diligence for them. They'll each want revenue numbers a specific way, growth numbers another way, customers another way, and so on. You will kill yourself organizing information in a bespoke fashion for every investor. So don't.

Leverage the associate. This is their job, after all: to crunch things and create a point of view called an investment memo. Make *them* do the work. Create a Dropbox folder with at most a few items in it. And make sure that the information is presented in the way you want. Investors ask you to break revenue down by logo? Do it, but don't send them the logos. Anonymize it. Logos are your secret and investors will call them. **ARR** doesn't look good annualized? Make it quarterly and provide them the sum instead of a line item detail. Find a way to tell the story you want or don't tell that story at all. If data doesn't serve you, don't provide it. Put information into PDFs, not spreadsheets. Invest time in getting graphs just right; it's a talent and when you see a good graph, the conclusion hits you over the head and you move on. Investors are sheep. Shepherd them.

Rule #9: Always answer the question *you* want to answer. I've said it before and I'll say it again. I live and die by this rule, even to the point where I will call out objections before they're raised because if I do that, I control the narrative. During one fundraise, we had a weird data point that demanded explanation. We didn't have a good answer, but instead of hiding it, we decided to call it out. So during the pitch, when we hit the "up and to the right" revenue graph, we said, "You know? You see that spike there? That was our first enterprise deal. And you're probably thinking that we should have raised then. You're right. We should have. But we're here now and so let me share how much we've learned about the enterprise since and how that's now a part of our sales cycle blah blah blah." By calling out the objection and reframing it, you own the narrative. This is also a prime example of why practice runs with investors you don't care about are so critical. They'll ask all the same questions later-stage folks will. The prep is worth its weight in gold.

In practice, this is not a skill that most of us founders have at the beginning nor one that comes naturally. Investors are very, very good at thinking before they speak, so good that in one universe I'd argue their full-time job is masking what they're really saying, which makes sense. This is their job. Founders, in contrast, are less so. We are typically young, hungry, and brash. Or we're maladjusted engineers who LARP on the weekends for fun. In any case, we're human and untrained at that. If investors think too much and founders not enough (at least until they're more long-in-the-tooth), you can see what kind of odds that creates, especially early on. The only thing I can say is that, knowing this, your job is, again, to control the narrative as much as possible. Dig, perceive, try to figure out what the question under the question is, and only then answer. Answer a question with a question until you've figured it out. You can't do your job unless you understand, much like a diplomat.

Rule #10: Pre-term sheet diligence (technical or otherwise) can drag you down. Don't let it. We're talking max two pitches, one call with your CTO, a few customer references, and then a partner meeting. If it's anything more than that, something is wrong and the investor is stuck on a point. Identify that point or move on.

Rule #11: There is no such thing as "getting investor feedback." *No such thing*. If you are talking to an investor, you are raising. I don't care if it's a fifteen minute coffee a year before the raise. *You are raising*. If you insist on doing this, you must carefully map out what you can and cannot say. Investors will insist that "we need to develop a relationship because we only invest in founders we truly know." They will use clichés that sound great on coffee mugs. They are not saying it because they want to get to know you. They are saying it because they want to (wait for it) stay as close to a deal for as long as possible so that they can defer saying yes. The longer they wait to say yes, the more they have mitigated their risk. They are *not your friends*. They care about one thing and one thing only and that is their investment return. There are very few investors that I would call friends.

Now, does it help that you can call eleven investors up the moment you decide to raise and say, "Yo, want the inside track on this round?" Sure! But you can get fifty more lined up right after that. Does it help that you have gotten to know people so you have a sense of their personality? Sure! But guess what? People change and investors are slick and they *do not care about you*. They care about their return. Why give them the chance to get close to you when it does really nothing to help you in the long run and everything to help them?

I'll admit this advice has bitten me in the ass before. It's made fundraising more difficult at times, and I've chosen bad or ineffectual investors because of it. I also have the same problem with investors whom I've known for a decade. Somewhere in the middle is most likely accurate, but remember: If you're going to go out for coffee, you must invest time in architecting what you're saying. They have long memories and zero hesitancy ignoring your emails if they don't like what they hear over coffee.

Rule #12: Disqualify quickly. Very quickly. Or get rejected quickly. Very quickly. I don't care which way it is, but get the breakup over with so you can focus on the ones who matter. One of my favorite things to teach sales hires was to get the prospect off the phone as quickly as possible by disqualifying them. If the prospect really needs your software, they'll come back. And if they don't, they'll say thanks but no thanks. The same holds true with VCs.

Remember, if a founder's job is to cut through thc bullshit and discover the real reason for a rejection or extra work (a skill that takes time to develop), then a VC's job is to string you along for as long as possible to mitigate their risk of committing capital to a failing business. Unless you're in a frothy market or you've built a transporter from *Star Trek*, nobody is going to tell you the truth. They'll "stay in touch" or "check in" or "I'm traveling for the next two weeks but how about then" or they'll ghost.

Humans do not like to be uncomfortable, and venture capitalists are no exception. To say no and give the real reason why requires being uncomfortable. Think about the last time you broke up with someone. Did you actually say to them that you thought you could be okay with the fact that they washed cars for a living but really you just wanted to be taken out to a fancy meal without worrying if they'd be able to pay rent the next day? No. You didn't. You said that you weren't ready for something right now or that you thought they were incredible and asked if you could be friends. You did that because you didn't want to hurt them, but what that really means is that you didn't want to be uncomfortable.

Investors do that too. When they say they don't believe in the market or that the valuation is too high or that they're not sure the tech is defensible, know that all of that is bogus. You need to hear a sentence like, "We judge companies in three areas: team, go-to-market, and product. We think you and your co-founder are great and the product is built solidly. But we disagree with your approach in selling top down to the Fortune 500 and think there's a bigger opportunity in going to mid-market first. Furthermore, you didn't seem to be open to the idea of other approaches and you deserve an investor who agrees with your vision." *That's* a real rejection. You'll never get it.

In summary: Assume the investor consistently avoids sharing what they think, from first meeting to exit. It's a truth in the world, like death and taxes. Find a way to get them to reject you or dump them yourselves.

INVESTOR VIEW: KNOW YOUR FOUNDER

Of the more than twenty emailed pitches from founders I get each week, I am initially interested in four or five, end up talking to two or three, and only invest in zero or one. On average, I invest in a new company every two months. For every twenty-five companies I am curious about, I will weed out twenty-four.

Deciding which companies to invest in is where a VC makes or breaks their fund. If you're good at investing in companies but bad at helping them afterward, you'll still make money. If you're bad at investing but good at helping, you'll lose money. Picking is the cornerstone of venture capital.

These are the decisions that keep me up at night. With every investment I know I'll probably lose my money, but there's an outside chance the company will become big. I lie in bed trying to predict what will happen. Sometimes, in a half-dream state, I start to believe I *can* predict what will happen.

If I could really predict the future, there would be easier ways to make money.

There's a temptation to just keep putting the decision off and seeing what happens with the company in the meantime. This is especially strong when part of the company's pitch is that they have a customer "ready to sign" a contract with them. Will the customer sign, or won't they? This is a crucial piece of data.

But there's only so long a founder will wait, and there's only so long it's ethical to keep a founder waiting. If you string them on too long, you might be keeping them from looking for money from someone else. I've known plenty of founders who mistook investor indecision for interest and stopped looking elsewhere only to have that investor eventually say no. VCs are a no until they actually say yes.

Make a decision. Invest or don't invest. You won't know if you're wrong for at least a year, and you won't know if you're right for a long time after that. "Lemons ripen before pearls" is the old VC saying; startups that are going to fail will fail before, sometimes long before, the ones that succeed.

Sometimes VCs think an idea is riskless, but this is an illusion. There's no such thing as a free lunch, but that's okay. Instead of wasting my time looking for riskless ways to double my money, I look for a one-in-a-hundred chance of making five hundred times my money. That's what VCs do.

Once I've narrowed the companies down to that one that I want to invest in, I start to pitch the founder. I tell them why I love their idea and how I think they are the perfect person to build their company. I tell them how I can help and how I will interact with them. Then I tell them the kinds of terms I was thinking of: price, board composition, how much I can invest, and so on. If we can agree, I send them a term sheet, memorializing all the terms.

While I'm doing all this—the sourcing, the talking, the research, the meetings—I'm talking to the founder about what I'm hearing and trying to figure out if they are the right person. And, the hardest question: Can I trust them? Are they someone I can build a strong relationship with over time?

The longer you interact with the founder before you make the investment, the better you will know them. But you have to balance how long you take doing this against the danger some other VC will make a decision to invest more quickly. Most VCs take as much time as they think they can, more when the market is slower and less when the market is hot. Founders complain that VCs delay and delay, and they do. If they have the choice of making the investment with more information versus making it with less, they'll always choose more. It just makes sense. The best thing a founder can do about it is help the VC get comfortable with them, so the VC is as excited as the founder about getting the deal done.

Getting to know the founder before you invest is the only way to make sure you're making a good investment. More important than competitive / market analysis, financial modeling, and due diligence. And it not only means you are making a better investment, it is, in itself, an investment in the future.

RELATIONSHIPS LEAD TO OPPORTUNITIES

Some years ago I invested in the first round of a new company. It soon showed some real promise and had the opportunity to raise more money from some of the best venture firms in the world. The catch was that the various buyers—the new investors and the existing investors that had pro rata rights—wanted to buy more equity than the founders wanted to sell. The founders had to make some hard decisions about who they would sell the new equity to. I let them know I was interested and they said, "You've been really helpful, and we'd love for you to own more of the company." The shares I bought then became very valuable when the company went public a few years later. I would not have seen that gain without the good relationship.

FOUNDER VIEW: DILIGENCE IS POWER

When you're in the wooing phase, venture capitalists will spend a ton of time discussing how helpful they can be. They can introduce you to *so many* prospects, candidates, and advisors. They'll talk about their internal go-to market team that can cure whatever is ailing your sales motion. They'll advertise free McKinsey or Bain help, same thing for their **retained search** firm. They will overwhelm you with how much research they've done on your space (test this; they're undoubtedly not experts, and in my entire career

I've met exactly two associates who knew their stuff, as it related to my company's space, cold). Oh, and don't forget about their promised (and fictional) monthly panel where you present to a captive audience of [INSERT C-SUITE TITLE HERE] that will of course buy your product.

None of these things happen. Even firms that profess to be tops in this aren't. Sorry. Investors can be useful, although probably not in the ways you think and certainly not in the ways they publicize.

They are typically good at one thing and one thing only. For example, one of my early investors had the best Seed stage program I've ever experienced. Their community and the way they invest in that competency gets founders access to other founders who have been through it before to learn from them. They eliminate as many barriers as possible to helping their portcos learn from each other. And because they've had a number of companies grow quite large and maintained a board seat during that time, they can guide. Do they excel at enterprise-level customer introductions or have an insane network of salespeople? Not really, but others might. Find the one thing you can count on.

And if there is something to remember, investors have a narrative, just like founders do! It's your job as the steward of your business to (1) cut through that narrative so that you can (2) put them to work. This ideally happens before taking their money, though sometimes it can only happen after. So often founders don't do their own diligence—in hiring, with investors, researching term sheets, everything. This is a *huge mistake* and I'm not quite sure why it happens. Why wouldn't you want to know as much as possible about the person with whom you're about to make some sort of contract?

Founder power comes from knowledge. I have never once turned down another founder asking for help or my thoughts, and have never been turned down. We help one another. We just have to remember to ask. You acquire that knowledge by picking up the phone, going to coffee meetings, cold-emailing folks. You get it by shamelessly asking your lawyer's college roommate's boss for help. Someone took money from the person you're raising from. Someone fired the person to whom you're about to extend an offer. Someone knows something that nobody else does. Find them.

I've messed this up many times before. I hired an executive who hadn't lasted a year at each of their two prior companies. This person was great early on and faded later, big time. I waited far too long to terminate, against a cacophony of voices I should have listened to. Did this person not last at these companies for the reasons they said? Absolutely. Was it probably also for other reasons that I encountered as the company started scaling? For sure. I didn't call around as aggressively as I should have. That's on me. At the same time, when I've diligenced investors and found out all the salient points, including that they frequently fire their founders, I've still signed that term sheet. This is all to say that information isn't a panacea but it certainly does mean your decision is well-informed. And that's the job of a founder: making the best decision possible with the information available to you at the time.

I'll give you an example of an investor relationship I have that I believe is set up to be a successful one. By successful, I don't mean we're besties or that I have any illusions about his priorities. By successful I mean that we've been through enough frank conversations that I believe (1) he'll stand up to assholes, (2) he won't shy away from a difficult conversation (and might even instigate it himself), and (3) we actually vaguely like each other enough such that I would want to have a drink with him after a board dinner.

This person is an investor at a Tier 1 firm and, believe it or not, has never invested in any of my companies. I've pitched him at least three separate times, and in each instance, it didn't work out (term sheet timing issues, too much drama, not enough traction). I'm sure there were a half dozen other reasons; some were ours and some were his.

The relationship is both transactional and pleasurable. There are no illusions between us. We've spoken plainly and in depth as to why a deal never happened. Great example: He decided to fund a competitor. I found out months later when the press release came out. This was the email thread:

From: Elizabeth Zalman
To: XX
Subject: really?

:(

From: XX
To: Elizabeth Zalman
Subject: Re: really?

Really. How are you? What are you up to these days? Sorry didn't give you a heads up… honestly wasn't sure that was the right move. Sorry if that was the wrong call! You still in NYC?

From: Elizabeth Zalman
To: XX
Subject: Re: really?

Honestly? It hurt my feelings to find out this way.

From: XX
To: Elizabeth Zalman
Subject: Re: really?

Thanks for letting me know how you feel. Clearly I should have given you a heads up and made the wrong decision.

He stayed true to his word and reached out to meet the next time he was in NYC, four months later. I gave him more shit, he apologized again and more profusely, and then we settled into witty banter. An hour later, the transaction was over. Why is this so significant? Why do I prefer this over the Seed investor relationship where it's often more personal? It's because there's no pretense. *Zero pretense.* Will we go into business together one day? Maybe, maybe not. But we're both going to put in the effort in order to keep that possibility open. Do I believe this investor will ever make a decision that is antithetical to the interests of his firm? Nope. Does that include, say, firing me if it came to it? Yes. But I believe I'll hear about it straight from him and he'll have a real reason for doing whatever he does. And that's the best you can ask for from a VC, I think.

Over my career, I've pitched to nearly every Tier 1 fund and most in Tier 2. I've got a long memory on certain things, and how VCs behave is one of them. I'd love to be able to list out exactly what I think about folks I've pitched or taken money from but I'll get sued for libel. Instead, just invite me out for coffee.

Some examples:

- A well-known corporate fund has a lead cybersecurity investor that everyone fears having on calls. If there is a deal with a whiff of security that someone else brought in, he'll block it. The firm is aware of the problem and doesn't deal with it, doesn't care to deal with it, or perhaps it's something else entirely.

- As my co-author has previously written, one of the top firms in the world brags about firing more than 50% of their founders. That's their brand.

- A no-longer-top-tier-fund steals decks by pretending they haven't signed a term sheet with your competitor.

- A fund known for incubating companies in-house and spinning them out pulls term sheets.

- A well-known VC who has a massive online presence through a ton of well-written content marketing is full of bluster and completely disingenuous. I know of at least one founder who took a term sheet from the firm on the condition that this investor wouldn't be the one to join their board.

On the flip side, VCs have short memories and will never remember how they acted in a meeting. They'll email you for every round subsequent to the one in which you first met, not remembering anything about the prior interaction and certainly not their behavior.

During my last Series A, my co-founder and I were introduced by an existing investor to a general partner at a Tier 1 fund. These two men sat together on the board of a company that has since gone public. Ten minutes into the meeting, the GP said that he didn't invest in "anything not open source" and asked why we weren't open source. Our jaws dropped. Did you even look us up? Why did you agree to the intro and waste your fellow board member's time? We walked out, but not before wasting an hour of our lives.

Two years later, this investor reached out to me for our Series B saying how excited he was about what we were doing and I wanted to write back, "So do you not have your open source thesis anymore?" I didn't though, because guess what? Investors get to be assholes with zero self-awareness. Some founders do, too, I suppose. There are plenty of asshole founders who are terrible humans who become billionaires on a regular basis, and they're forgiven their sins, just like investors are. But most founders can't pull that off. Most of us have to be on our best behavior. If you're female, Black, Asian, anything but hetero and white and male . . . well then, you must be on your best behavior every moment of every day and probably also while you sleep.

HOW TO BLOW OFF STEAM WHILE PITCHING TO AN ASSHOLE

It can be frustrating to be patient, gracious, and present on fundraising calls while the investor gets to behave however they want to.

In this case, the person in question was the aforementioned cybersecurity investor, who was at a firm well known for vicious partner politics. This person had already decided to block the deal because it had been brought in by a partner they didn't like. They listened so little and talked so much during the pitch that my co-founder and I got bored and devolved to passing notes as if we were in high school social studies.

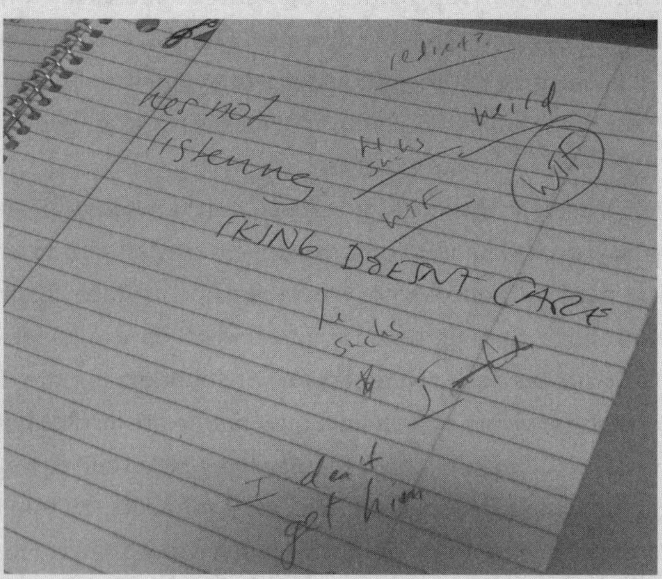

What's the point of all this exposition, you ask? What do I do? Well, as soon as you start fundraising, you *must* also walk the parallel path that is diligence. VCs will do diligence on you and your business—in the form of the data room, back channel to ex-workers and employees, your current investors—and you need to do the same on them and their firm. You might find that moment that actually gets you to turn down the term sheet. You might discover nothing nefarious at all and feel really good about things. Reality will end up being somewhere in the middle: a founder or two will share horror stories but couch them in things being "overall pretty good."

Know that I'm an advocate for diligence and yet I also believe you can never really know someone. There are the moments that are the leap of faith that is the relationship. As a founder, you do the best with the information you have, make a decision, and then fight like hell for every single right that exists in documents you're about to sign.

INVESTOR VIEW: WANT FOUNDERS TO SUCCEED

I was a much better investor after I was a startup founder. Seeing the process of fundraising from the other side of the table is one reason. VCs were arrogant, they were often dismissive, they had no qualms making me fly across the country to have coffee with them even when they had no intention of entertaining an investment in my company. I dealt with all these things because I knew I was building a network for the future.

But investors don't have to be this way. *You* don't have to be that way.

Once you've made contact with the entrepreneur, be professional. Respond promptly, honestly, and thoughtfully to their outreach (even if you don't intend to invest; see earlier). I know it's not always possible, given the number of pitches you might see. Tell them why you're passing, if you are. If they look promising but are just not in your sweet spot, offer to forward their email to another VC who might be interested. If their company is the type of thing you might invest in but there's something wrong with the pitch, respond with a longer email telling them exactly what rubbed you the wrong way. Be constructive. Some founders are just looking for affirmation and this pisses them off, but do it anyway.

If you meet with the entrepreneur, don't call their baby ugly. Be careful how and when you say no. Be mindful of their time and be encouraging about their willingness to take the risk of starting a company. If you say no to someone because they are starting a company outside of your field—because it is, say, consumer-facing when you do B2B—there are no hard feelings, and when someone they know starts a B2B company, they will send them to you. But if you take the pitch and then say no, founders can take it personally.

Talk to founders with an open mind. Don't be a pushover, just give them the opportunity to try and convince you. Some investors go into the first meeting looking to shoot ideas down as quickly as they can. This, obviously, rubs founders the wrong way. Almost every company I've worked with started with an idea that had to be changed as they explored it, so bad ideas are clearly not entirely disqualifying. If I meet someone who has a 75% decent idea for a company, I work with them to get it closer to 100%. Sometimes we can get there and sometimes I have to say no. But I am on their side, trying to find a way to make it work.

FOUNDER VIEW: CRUSH THAT SALE

Fundraising is just a sale. And you are a salesperson. You may think you're not, but you become one the moment you put on the founder mantle. Find the prospects, pitch them, get them to agree in principle to a deal, then get that in blood. You do that with smart thinking, storytelling, testing, and FOMO. Never blink. And as you're doing that, you're dialing for the information that could save your company, your life.

Go forth and conquer those pesky investors. *Crush them.*

KEY TAKEAWAYS

FOUNDER	INVESTOR
Founders have much more power during the fundraising process than they think.	VCs inevitably have an information advantage during the fundraising process. This can lead to mistrust between founder and investor.
A fundraise is nothing but a sale. To cut through the noise, you must have a strong narrative, rigorous methodology, and chutzpah.	VCs need founders as much as founders need them. VCs make themselves hard to pitch as a way to prequalify founders.
A founder's job is to get to a yes or no as quickly as possible. Everything else is a waste of time (including spending time with VCs).	Investors need to spend as much time as possible with founders before they invest.
Knowledge is power; diligence investors as if your life depends on it.	Good VCs must make decisions without enough data, be able to form and maintain relationships with their founders, and want the founders they invest in to succeed.

3

TERMS

INVESTOR VIEW: CONTRACTS AREN'T JUST LEGAL DOCUMENTS, THEY'RE AGREEMENTS

One morning, early in my investment career, my boss walked into my office and found me rereading one of our investment contracts. He asked me what I was doing, and I told him I was having trouble with a founder and wanted to make sure I knew what our legal rights were. "If you're relying on the contract," he said, "you've already lost. Go see him and work it out in person." Three hours later I was on a plane to SFO. I took the founder out to dinner and drinks, and by the time I boarded the red-eye home, we were friends again.

Contracts are wonderful things. They put down in black and white (and unambiguously, if you have good lawyers) what you and the company have agreed to. If, in the future, there is some disagreement, you can point to the contract. A founder once called me and told me my firm should give some of our equity back to the company. "Why would I do that?" I asked. He said, "*I* did all the work. Why should *you* make so much money?" I pointed out that when we invested, he willingly—eagerly, even—sold us a piece of the company. "Look," I said, "I have the contract we both signed in front of me, I can send you a copy if you've lost yours." He grumbled a bit but never brought it up again. I wasn't threatening to sue him, I was just reminding him that we had both agreed to the same thing.

Contracts are important in the same way that good fences make good neighbors: If boundaries are clear, everyone can get along. But if someone decides to simply ignore the contract, it's very hard to remedy. Lawsuits are expensive, take a long time, and tend to destroy more value than either side stands to gain. Relying on the contract—in the sense that you ask a judge, arbitrator, and/or jury to decide what it says—that's what my boss meant when he said you've already lost.

As an investor, you can't afford to be too aggressive anyway. Word gets around (everyone in this industry is an inveterate gossip), and a VC who plays rough quickly finds that the best founders don't want their money anymore and other VCs don't want to work with them. VCs are playing a repeated game; they always have to keep the next deal in mind. This is also why it's dangerous to take money from non-VCs, like carpetbagging hedge funds or opportunistic corporates, who don't play for the long term. If they decide to leave the business, they'll have no qualms about squeezing the last dime from everyone in sight.

VCs can screw founders only once before they get a reputation for it. This doesn't stop them from continuing to invest or even getting lucky once in a while, but it limits their access to the best founders, the ones who do their due diligence.

The same goes for founders; they can only screw VCs once, but in their case once is probably enough. A *successful* founder never has to raise money from VCs again in their lives. They do not have to worry about VCs getting angry at them the same way VCs have to worry. When founders do the right thing, it's because they are the kind of people who do the right thing. I look for founders I can trust. I avoid founders who are get-rich-quick types, who care only about their own success.

What constitutes screwing someone else versus just playing hardball depends on what you have agreed to. With most agreements, you sit down, hash it out, and shake hands. But since a VC-startup relationship can last ten years or more, memories fade and details get distorted. If the agreement is down on paper, in a contract, that can't happen.

THE DOCS

When we talk about the "contract" or "docs" (i.e., documents), we are talking about the legal agreements that specify a venture capital investment into a startup. These docs are more than just a contract, they are a set of contracts and other legal documents that encompass all aspects of the raise. Every law firm does things slightly differently, but (with the caveat that I am not a lawyer) the standard set of documents includes the following:

STOCK PURCHASE AGREEMENT (THE SPA)

This describes how many shares of the company are being sold for what amount of money, but the meat of it is the "representations and warranties": the buyer and seller assuring each other that the things they said are true. The seller will rep to things like the truth of their financial statements and that they own their intellectual property, while the buyer will rep that they are actually allowed to buy the stock, and so on. The reps and warranties are usually heavily negotiated by the lawyers because if they're not true, the other side can sue to void the sale. This is pretty unusual in practice, but best to listen to your lawyers here.

VOTING AGREEMENT

The term sheet usually dictates who is on the board, and this agreement ensures everybody votes to make that happen. It also has the "drag along": If more than a certain percentage of the investors agree to sell the company, the rest have to agree also; they are "dragged along." This prevents holdouts from negotiating for more.

INVESTORS' RIGHTS AGREEMENT (THE IRA)

This is a grab bag of all the other things investors want:

- Right of first offer, sometimes called pro rata rights: Whatever percentage of the company the investor owned before the offering, they get to buy that percentage of the shares sold in the offering. That is, if you currently own 20% of a company, and they are selling new stock for $5 million, you have the right to purchase $1 million, or 20%, of it. This way you have the same percentage of ownership before and after the round (although, if the **stock option pool** is increased, you will suffer some dilution).
- Information rights: Investors must be sent specified information.
- Registration rights: The ability for investors to either force a public offering of shares or have their shares made eligible to sell on an exchange after an IPO.

All these rights are usually only given to "Major Investors." This is negotiated and is typically the larger investors or leads. If you're not a Major Investor, you might be able to negotiate some of this (probably just information rights and pro rata rights) into a Side Letter agreement or a Management Rights Letter (MRL).

RIGHT OF FIRST REFUSAL AND CO-SALE AGREEMENT (ROFR)

This says that if founders or investors sell their shares, certain investors or the company have the right to buy them. This prevents having unwanted shareholders in the company (a competitor, perhaps.) The co-sale allows investors to sell some of their own shares if the founder is selling. The co-sale right is commonly called the tag-along, so as to pleasingly rhyme with drag-along.

THE CERTIFICATE OF INCORPORATION (THE COI) AND BYLAWS

The COI is filed in the state of incorporation (almost always Delaware, because the law there is pro-corporation; and, btw, the corporation is almost always a C-corporation) and says how many shares there are, what happens if the company gets dissolved or liquidated, and so on. This has to be amended when more shares are created, but the significant clauses will describe how preference and anti-dilution work for preferred shares. The bylaws may also be filed with the state: They specify how the company is run at the board level, so they may have things from the term sheet such as what needs to be voted on by the board (approving the annual budget, selling the company, and the like).

OTHER DOCS

Other things that are often included in the packet of docs are employment agreements for the founders and key employees; agreements to indemnify board members against lawsuits; the schedule of exceptions/disclosure schedule, which lists all the places where the company is not in compliance with the reps and warranties (and is the most important document in the whole set); the consent of the board to the transaction; and a consent of the existing shareholders to the new contracts (which supersede their own contracts). This is not a comprehensive list, but I think it covers the most important things.

Contracts are long and boring and full of boilerplate. Usually the important things in them—or at least the things that are not the exact same in every venture deal—can be summarized in a few pages. That summary is the first thing a VC hands to a founder after they've decided they would like to invest: a term sheet.

FOUNDER VIEW: TAKE YOUR TIME WITH THAT TERM SHEET

The term sheet is your future summarized in one and a half pages. It's super exciting to get. The most legendary way to get one is by having it presented at dinner, and I was lucky enough to have that experience. Either way, revel in the offer for a few minutes and then realize it's time to get to work.

INVESTORS HAVE THEIR WEAKNESSES

There are three things to keep in mind when the term sheet arrives, and these same three things mean different things to the founder and to the investor:

WHAT THE FOUNDER SHOULD THINK	WHAT THE INVESTOR IS THINKING
Everything is negotiable, starting now.	I really hope they just sign it because now I have to get this deal closed.
Time to call all the other funds in the mix to see if we can get even more offers!	I wonder how many other offers they have? Is mine competitive enough?
I'm in control.	How much more can I do to scare them into thinking I'm going to pull the term sheet so that they just sign it already?

First things first. Most founders will race to sign the term sheet and say, "We'll deal with any problems in the docs." Investors will push you to do that because they want to close the deal. *Wrong. Wrong wrong wrong wrong wrong.*

I'll say it again: *wrong*.

The term sheet is the template for your docs. This term sheet is a template for your relationship, a template to hand to your very expensive lawyers to create the docs. You do *not* want to defer hashing out key business points for when you're mired in gobs of legal jargon; you want them figured out up front. You don't accept a job offer without knowing the salary up front. You don't accept an offer on your condo without knowing if it's contingent on another sale. Why would you do anything differently here? If you defer that negotiation, the balance of power has now shifted back to the investor.

You may get scared at the thought of pushing back. That's natural. But it is better to walk away from a term sheet knowing it's not a good deal up front rather than to discover it in the middle of the long-form docs and having backed yourself against a wall because this fund is now your *only* option.

Sometimes that fear comes from the dates at the bottom of term sheets that say that the paper expires if you don't sign by then. Feel free to ignore them! This is a scare tactic. If you are engaged and negotiating in good faith, the date will be updated. Remember, the VC *wants* this term sheet to be signed. One lesson I relearn on every fundraise is that a term sheet can never have *enough* detail.

The second piece of power you have is that a term sheet is an actual written offer of your company's market value. That gives you license to go get a competing offer! The more options you have, the better, so go, quickly.

The way to do it is to call up everyone else in the mix and say, "Hey, we got a term sheet and we are negotiating it now. If you want to be a part of the round, I'll need a term sheet by end of day." They'll ask you what it says. Don't tell them. Shopping a term sheet isn't classy and there are ways to suggest what's in it by saying things like, "You must be within X and Y valuation" or "It's competitive." You may get folks to fight head-to-head for your deal, or another one may decide to follow rather than lead, or they say, "No, thank you," in which case they were never going to put in an offer anyway. All these outcomes are fantastic. Certainty in this moment is your friend.

I was in one deal in which we had signed a term sheet, and another fund (who had issued a term sheet that we rejected) marked up their own paper and sent it back to win the deal. They redlined all of their rights out, *just to win*. VCs are all about winning, and beating out another fund is no exception. That should show you how much flexibility there is in the process and that you shouldn't be scared. This is an example of founder power that you have and that they don't want you to know you have. Use it.

Now, you've probably heard horror stories of term sheets being pulled. It does happen. It's most likely for reasons outside of your control: markets have blown up (**LPs** unable to wire funds they don't have), the term sheet shouldn't have been issued in the first place (portfolio competition), personal conflict, or any number of other things.

During one fundraise, a Tier 1 firm pulled my term sheet three days before the close. It was a crazy deal to begin with as all early investors were going to get cashed out at a wonderful valuation. We were originally talking to one partner there that we liked but were switched at the last minute to a new, junior female partner because this fund liked the female-female narrative *and* this woman had a connection to one of our largest angel investors.

A week before the close, their accountant called me to ask if we'd consider truncating the share price from four significant digits to two. Four is standard. Moving to two would have meant redoing all docs, the entire cap table, and it seemed like the accountant was trying to pawn some wiring challenges off onto someone else (me). I said no. The new female partner leading the deal then called me to tell me I was "aggressive"—verbatim—and that they were pulling out.

Put aside everything else: A venture capital firm pulled a term sheet three days before the close because they chose to not have a conversation about something that they were upset about. One of my investors called her and she wouldn't even talk through the issue with him, someone who had known and worked with me for years. I'm not even going to touch the insanity of a female calling a female aggressive (that's two people now, including Jerry's story of my first fundraise in the Fundraising chapter); you can bet that doesn't happen to a man. In the aftermath, there was only one investor on my cap table that I'm aware of who proactively vowed to warn every founder who talked with that firm about what happened to me. One. I expected a low number, but one? This is a fantastic example of VCs being beholden to their peers and so keeping their mouths shut is in everyone's best interests. To me, it's simply disgusting.

YOU ARE STRONGER THAN YOU THINK

When the aforementioned term sheet was pulled, I was staying at Uncle Lenny's house in Florida. I went to bed and woke up in the middle of the night, beyond nauseated. I proceeded to spend the next few hours sick.

In the morning, I heard Uncle Lenny getting ready to leave and called out to him for help. He came in and I told him what had happened. He said, "Lizzie, you'll be fine, it's just stress. Here's a Gatorade. I'm going golfing," turned on his heel, and left. Talk about putting things in perspective.

A few hours later, I sent an email to the cap table letting them know what had happened. One of our existing investors called immediately and said, "I'm going to ask you how you're doing in a second, but first things first: Does the company need any more money?"

Now *that* is an investor. Rephrased: I care about you, but I care about the company more, so let me make you feel good by making sure you know I care about both before I ask about the more important of the two. I'd be hard pressed to name a more perfect example of what I hope from an investor than that moment. I'd raise from him any day.

An investor pulling a term sheet at any point, but especially a few days before a close, leaves a company in dire straits. If the company is earlier in its life cycle, it's common knowledge to employees you're out raising because founders disappear for weeks on end (fundraising is a full-time job). When the sheet is pulled, the money you were banking on is now gone. You can't go back out and raise again immediately because you were just out and that's incredibly weak signaling to the market. Just imagine the conversation:

VC: Didn't we just talk to you and you turned us down because you had an offer?

Founder: Yeah.

VC: And you want what from me now?

Founder: Uhhhh . . .

Exactly. You're going to get raked over the coals on valuation and/or your reputation will be ruined because seriously what did you do to get a term sheet pulled (always the founder's fault, never the VC's).

What do you do? You take a breather for six months from fundraising. It's just long enough for all the investors you pitched previously to forget you were out while pulling together a story that's plausible for when you go back out again. "Oh, yes, we did talk in March but I decided to press pause. As we were in the early stages of raising, we [DID THIS THING] that unlocked a fundamentally [NEW REVENUE STREAM] and I decided that a few more months meant a much better business, and have I mentioned that our valuation has doubled?" Now that's a story. Put your head down and continue building a great business.

This story is the exception, not the rule. I share it because even in these most horrid of moments, you must keep your wits about you. Act rationally when negotiating the term sheet with that mythical, magical investor you're *dying* to have on the cap table and when you're trying to pick up the pieces because some holier-than-thou lawyer tries to sneak in a contrary term at the last moment.

Decide your future on the merits of the offer and your back channel alone; nothing else. You do that and you'll be fine.

INVESTOR VIEW: TERM SHEET TERMS

Term sheets aren't contracts, and they're not legally binding. But you, the investor, have a moral obligation to honor them once you've given one to a founder, within limits. If it turns out the founder hasn't been upfront with you during the process, has lied, or hasn't disclosed vital information, then you don't have to go through with it. But, by giving them a term sheet, you are asking them to stop raising money from anyone else and move on to the next stage: getting the investment papered and signed. If you pull it, you can easily kill the company.

As Liz notes, the startup founder is not under the same moral obligation: if you give them a term sheet, they are not morally obligated to take it. Some VC firms try to force this moral obligation by having the founder sign the term sheet, noting their acceptance. This isn't usually legally binding, but it puts the founder in the same place as the investor. Some firms even ask that the founder sign by a certain date, usually within a few days. No one wants to do the work needed to put out a term sheet just to find out they're a stalking horse. More importantly, if a venture capitalist had to convince their partnership to back the deal, going back and telling them the startup used them to get a better deal makes them look incompetent.

Better than a drop-dead date, though, is talking to the founder beforehand about what they would accept and not formally issuing a term sheet until you've come to an agreement. If the founder won't do this, then you have not sold the founder on your value and are not the preferred investor. It's okay to walk away and try to do better on the next deal. Giving a term sheet to a founder before you have agreed on a price is heads you win, tails I lose.

Not that agreeing on price is easy. Founders want a higher valuation and investors a lower one, of course. But the real problem is there isn't any way to estimate the objective value. How much is the company worth? If the company needs $2 million to get to the next **milestone**, the founder has to give up some ownership. If the founders can keep this dilution low as the company raises round after round, then they will own a larger chunk of it when it finally comes time to exit.

DILUTION

Dilution is a tricky concept, so here's a simplified example of an imaginary company (TechCo) raising two rounds of capital. The company has one founder, Susan, who has decided there are one million shares in the company (it doesn't matter much what this number is, only the ownership percentages really matter).

Before the first round, the cap table looks like this:

SHAREHOLDER	SHARES	OWNERSHIP
Susan	1,000,000	100%

Susan then convinces VC 1 to invest $2 million in the company at a **pre-money valuation** of $8 million. Because there are one million shares before the round, this works out to $8 per share, so VC 1 buys 250,000 shares.

SHAREHOLDER	SHARES	OWNERSHIP
Susan	1,000,000	80%
VC 1	250,000	20%
Total	1,250,000	100%

Susan's ownership percentage has shrunk. This is dilution.

After building the business for a year or two, TechCo needs more money, and Susan convinces VC 2 to put in $5 million at a $20 million pre-money. This works out to $16 per share ($20 million/1,250,000 shares) so VC 2 buys 312,500 shares.

SHAREHOLDER	SHARES	OWNERSHIP
Susan	1,000,000	64%
VC 1	250,000	16%
VC 2	312,500	20%
Total	1,562,500	100%

Susan has been diluted again, and VC 1 has also been diluted. Now, imagine that instead of this second round being at $20 million it was at a higher pre-money valuation, say $40 million. VC 2 buys shares at $32 per share and gets 156,250 shares.

SHAREHOLDER	SHARES	OWNERSHIP
Susan	1,000,000	71%
VC 1	250,000	18%
VC 2	156,250	11%
Total	1,406,250	100%

Because the valuation of the company was higher in the second scenario, there is less dilution and Susan and VC 1 both own a larger percentage of the company. Note that in non-imaginary situations there are other complications, like the stock option pool and early investors taking pro rata.

Some investors prefer to value the company post-money. Post-money is just the pre-money valuation plus the value of the money invested (with adjustments to compensate for increasing the option pool during the round). This has advantages and disadvantages, but the one thing that everyone should focus on is the final price per share. When the company one day goes public (fingers crossed) the amount of money you make is determined by what price per share you paid when you bought and what price per share you get when you sell. Nothing else.

The really wealthy founders ended up really wealthy either because they raised very little money and sold very little of their company (Bill Gates, for instance) or because they raised money at very high valuations (Mark Zuckerberg). Either of these paths is viable, but VCs will push back on both: They would rather invest more money than less, and they would rather invest at low valuations than high.

VCs pretty much guess at valuation. They sort of know the range of valuations that will produce good results, but this range is a wide one. I invest very early in companies, when they have the most risk, and my valuation analyses often result in something like "$8 million, plus or minus $6 million." It's just impossible to analytically pinpoint how much a company is worth when they're raising venture capital. Founders tend to be more optimistic and pick the higher end of the range while investors tend to look for less risk and pick the lower end of the range. Neither really knows who is right, so picking the price becomes a negotiation.

Paul Graham of **Y Combinator** once said investors shouldn't worry too much about the price they buy a company's stock for because the ones that fail end up being worth nothing, and the ones that succeed end up being worth a huge multiple of the price paid. This is excellent advice . . . for Y Combinator, who already owns a piece of the company. But it ignores the obvious fact that if you always bid at the high end of the range, you're going to, on average, do a lot worse than if you bid lower.

If multiple VCs put down a term sheet, the highest price usually wins. And whoever wins, having paid more than anyone else will pay, has probably overpaid. This is just a variety of the **winner's curse**. The more VCs that bid on the company, the more the winner overpaid.

How do you avoid overpaying? Investors use a few strategies. First, they know what the market price is: what other VCs are paying for similar companies. Market prices in venture are especially volatile, but it still helps to have some idea what the other bidders are thinking.

Second, they talk to other VCs they think might be interested and partner to offer a term sheet. If you are interested in the company, there are undoubtedly a dozen other VCs who would also be interested. By partnering with some of them, you pool your knowledge, letting you come up with a better estimate of what the company is really worth.

Partnering with other investors in a **syndicate** has other advantages, for both sides. If you're only committing part of the round, then you might be taking the risk the founder can't raise the rest. They might be spending your money not on building a product, but on raising more money. (Term sheets often have the amount the investor will invest as well as the aggregate proceeds of the round. It's up to the founder to find the rest of the money, though a good lead investor should be able to help.)

It also helps to have multiple investors if things aren't going quite to plan and the company has to raise an **inside round**. The more checkbooks there are around the table, the better the chance the money gets raised.

Third, they offer things besides money. Sometimes this is just the reputation for investing in winners. If the VC is Sequoia Capital or the like, founders will often take their money even if the price is lower. Sequoia has had so many winning companies, they must have some secret way of influencing outcomes, right? Founders know this is magical thinking, but they still fall for it.

Some VCs also offer in-house services like recruiting and public relations. For a founder with no expertise in these things, this is a powerful draw. Never mind that the in-house expertise will almost certainly be concentrated on the companies that are showing the most promise (that is, the ones that need it the least). At the other end of the spectrum are the firms that promise to just leave the founder alone. They won't insist on a board seat, they promise not to call every week for a check-in, and so on. These firms appeal to the founders who are pretty sure they don't need any help whatsoever, despite never having started or managed anything before.

And last is the inside round. VCs who are already investors will preemptively offer to fund the next round. This will almost certainly be at a lower price than the founder could get from a new VC, but it saves them the time they would have spent fundraising, time they can use to keep building the business.

Price is the primary wildcard in a term sheet, but you'll have to negotiate some other things as well. Even if the terms are incredibly fair, most founders have never seen a term sheet before and some of the stuff may seem outlandish.

CONVERTIBLE NOTES AND SAFES

Many early-stage deals are done these days with convertible notes or SAFEs (Simple Agreements for Future Equity). The former is essentially just a loan made by the investor, but it also can be converted into equity at the next fundraise at a discounted price per share.

An investor might, through a convertible note, lend a company $1 million with the right to have this money buy $1 million of shares in the next round at a price 20% lower than the rest of the round. There might also be a maximum price, usually expressed as a valuation. So the note might be $1 million with a 20% discount and a $5 million cap.

SAFEs are a middle ground between notes and real equity. An investor gives the company $1 million, which automatically becomes equity in the next round, in the same way as a note. SAFEs can be downloaded for free and customized by the user, no lawyer required at all.

Both SAFEs and convertible notes are notably simpler than equity contracts and cost far less in legal fees to put in place. The price is that they do not give investors most of the needed protections discussed in this chapter. In any case, they are both stopgaps until the company raises an equity round.

The most important terms after price are how the spoils are divided if the company is sold, and who controls it in the interim. I will leave control for the next chapter, but in addition to price, here I'll talk about **preferred stock**, founder vesting, information rights, and pro rata rights. Most of the other terms will either be boilerplate or the kind of things the lawyers fight about but that make no real difference either way (like whether dividends are accrued and at what rate: In my thirty years of doing this I have never seen this make a difference). Regardless of their importance, every one of these terms has stood the test of time and survived the competition between hundreds of funds, both "founder friendly" and otherwise, because each has a reason.

Almost all VCs insist on buying preferred stock. This means that if things go badly and there isn't enough money left to pay both the VCs and the founders, the VCs get their money back first. Once they've gotten their money back, the founder starts to get some. This sometimes seems wildly unfair to founders, but it is almost universal. I have a theory that every sentence in every contract is the result of someone getting screwed because their contract didn't have that sentence. Under this theory, preferred stock came about after some crafty founder got a VC to buy 20% of a company for $5 million one day, and dissolved the company the next day. That founder got their 80% of the $5 million for doing nothing. The VC got back $1 million. Preference solves for that. As to fairness, what preference ensures is that the founder makes money only if the investor makes money. It aligns their interests.

There are other ways to align interests, such as causing founders to "re-vest" into the shares they own in the company. That is, the founders "earn" their 80% over four years. This tends to seem unfair to founders, since they own all their shares outright just before the investment. Founder re-vesting is valuable when the founder does something entirely unexpected, like decide to retire to Costa Rica or get arrested for a felony. These are edge cases, but you get the idea. You are valuing the business based on the founder and their team's future work, but you are giving them the money today. This mismatch introduces risk that founder re-vesting might mitigate.

The other term that bears on valuation is the option pool. Investors will often require the company to increase the stock option pool to a certain size. You negotiate this in the term sheet because you know the company is going to have to give out options in order to hire the right people. The board could always increase the pool later, but by stipulating the pool upfront you can avoid later arguments about dilution (issuing options, like selling new shares, dilutes all existing holders of shares).

Information rights allow you to know how the company is doing. You need to be able to have some handle on whether the company might make you money in the future or not, so you can allocate your time and follow-on capital. Without information rights, the company has no obligation to tell you how they're doing. This seems pretty innocuous, but many investors don't have information rights in the companies they invest in, and most early-stage investors lose them after a subsequent round.

IN PRACTICE, EVERYTHING YOU NEGOTIATED IS TEMPORARY

When I was just starting out as an investor, one of the things that surprised me was that new rounds have new contracts, and new contracts can change all the rights you have negotiated. You can always refuse to sign the new contracts, though you might get dragged along if you're a smaller investor, but this might mean no new funding for the company. You don't want to be known as the investor who put a company out of business because you were stubborn about information rights.

It's worth noting that later-stage investors can—and will usually try to—take contractual rights away from earlier-stage investors. If you're an early-stage investor, you have to guard against this. Often, your only real protection is having the founder, who has more negotiating leverage with new investors than you do, stick up for you.

Some founders don't like their investors having information rights because they worry the VC might share that information with competitors. Sometimes VCs end up having an investment in companies that compete with each other, either because they thought it wouldn't be a problem or because the two companies started out not competing but one or both of them changed their business model, ending up as competitors. I've never known a VC to give inside information about a company they invested in to a competitor, because it would both affect their reputation and hurt one of their own investments, but I can understand the fear. Founders have to trust their investors not to share secrets, and the investors might not have earned their trust yet.

Founders often flip this on its head and tell investors that instead of having contractual information rights, investors should just trust *them* to always be open and honest. This is nice, in theory. But there are many situations where trust ends up not being enough. The most obvious is when either the partner monitoring the investment at the VC firm changes (because they leave, or whatever) or the company decides to put a new CEO in to replace the founder. When the people change, a trusting relationship has to be built from scratch. Getting contractual information rights is a much better bet, especially for VCs who invested early in the company's life. There may not be an opportunity to interact enough with the new management to build trust.

There are several ways VCs ask for information rights. Taking a board seat or observer seat on the board of directors seems the most like a win-win because the VC gets information and the founder gets advice (but, again, see the Board of Directors chapter). Board updates tend to be pretty exhaustive, though management will sandbag when things aren't going well. Only the very best founders will tell you all the bad news you need to know. It's hard to be entirely honest with people who can fire you.

Second best is contractual information rights. These are okay, but information rights provide you with only limited information. Maybe you get to see the financial statements every quarter or, if you've really thought ahead, the **board decks**. But without the context you get from talking to the founder or CEO, it's hard to really know what's going on. Still, it's something.

Regardless of what you ask for in the term sheet, you should build a relationship with the founder. If they trust you, they will give you the inside story. You take them out for coffee and they fill you in. They will give you context around the financial information, and some view into what the financials don't show, such as the likelihood of landing a new customer or promising new products under development. If the founder trusts you, they will tell you what the other investor board members are saying, letting you know both how good these investors are as board members (informing how eager you should be to bring them into future deals) and what sorts of follow-on and exit pressure they are receiving.

First choice on information: all of these things. Second choice: information rights plus relationship, because you will probably lose the board seat in some future round anyway. You might also lose the information rights when you stop being a major investor, but it's something you can keep pushing for in every round and it might reasonably be given (because it's not that big a give).

The most immediate need for information rights comes when the company is raising a **follow-on round**. Sometimes the existing investors have the right to participate, and this can be a valuable opportunity. So valuable that you should negotiate your right to participate in the next round into the term sheet for the current round. These are the pro rata rights I mentioned previously.

Founders are often advised not to give this to investors, but I get it whenever I can and insist on it when I first invest in a company. My first investment is the riskiest because I don't know the company's future that well and I also don't know the founder that well. By the time of the second investment, though, I do know the founder well and, from that, I can infer how the company will do, to some extent. These follow-on investments usually have a much better risk-adjusted return. Pro rata rights also protect you from getting screwed by later investors in a **down round**.

IT'S HARD TO MAKE DECISIONS WITHOUT INFORMATION

One company I was an investor in was raising an inside round and I was invited to participate. I did not have a relationship with the CEO, because they had replaced the original founder. I also did not have information rights, so I had no idea how the company was doing.

I could not get the CEO to return my calls. I called one of the big investors, whom I had introduced to the company—it's hard to find good startups, so if you introduce an investor to a company and they find it appealing enough to invest in, you've done them a favor. But this VC told me, "It would be against our professional interests to let you know if we are investing in this round." So much for doing him a favor.

Luckily, a partner at another major investor in the deal was happy to tell me their thoughts, so I had enough information to make the right decision.

One last contentious term. The VC's legal fees are paid by the company. Founders often think this is unfair, and it does seem a bit like robbing Peter to pay Paul. But it's just easier for the investor to have the company pay the lawyer's fees. If, say, I organize a syndicate to invest in a company, then everyone in the syndicate uses the contracts my lawyer drafts. If I paid the lawyer myself, I'd have to go back to all the other investors in the syndicate and try to get them to pay their pro rata share of the fees. It would be a nightmare. Instead, I just have the investors put a bit more into the company and have the company pay.

And, frankly, it makes no difference: If the founder feels strongly about the investors' $30,000 legal bill in a $1 million round, then offer to raise the valuation by enough to compensate for it.

FOUNDER VIEW: THE TERMS FOUNDERS *REALLY* NEED TO CARE ABOUT

As Jerry said, most paragraphs in a term sheet should be fairly standard, especially at the early stage (such as **participating preferred** multiples), but there are a few key points that are critical for the founder to get right.

First, unlike my co-author and also unlike many founders, I am personally less concerned about things like information rights. I believe investors should have a right to know what's going on, and if I don't trust them not to speak, I should never have taken their money in the first place. Sending that information out may get unwieldy, but I've never run a company in secret and never will. The founder instinct tends to be one of self-preservation—"Why are they asking for this, are they going to send it to my competitor?"—but I believe you're better off sharing than not.

Jerry suggests that the highest valuation term sheet typically wins and he's probably right. Founders get overwhelmed by the high number and drift toward it. That's a mistake. You *must* look at the entire picture. As one investor once said to me (just like Paul Graham), "Liz, if you do this right, it's all a rounding error." This person would know; he also said, "Let me pay for drinks; money just shows up on my doorstep."

Of every term sheet I've signed in the past fifteen years, none of them were the highest valuation. Valuation is not board power is not ownership. Know the difference because that difference is your life. Don't lose sight of critical things like power just because a sexy valuation number is staring you in the face. Term sheets are typically plus or minus in-market. And if they're too high, you as the founder should acknowledge that. Because valuations are a bet on the future, everything can come crashing down if they're too high. To mitigate this risk, every time I raise I also run a parallel sales process. It might take the company off the market (most likely not), but most important, it validates or invalidates the value of the term sheet. High may be sexy but high may also set you up for failure.

Now, there's also a term that isn't customarily introduced unless the founder asks for it but can be negotiated in. Next to control, it may be the most important term you ask for. It's called a **co-sale right, exempt from the ROFR**. This gives founders the right to take some money off the table, an agreed-on percent of what they hold, typically in future financings (but sometimes elsewhere). No investor will introduce this because why would they want a founder to be able to cash out if the VC can't, but this is silly. Good investors should care about the health of their founders, and if a startup has been going on for the better part of a decade, some liquidity might ease a founder's mind. I know it did mine. Like many things that are possible in deals that VCs don't want you to know about, I originally heard about it through a co-founder's friend. So negotiate for the highest percent possible. Fifteen percent is outstanding. Don't accept less than 5%. Even if you're at the Seed stage, do it now.

The next term is related to but separate from founder re-vesting. Permit me a rant, first, because re-vesting is absurd. There are other ways to solve for it, ways that more rightfully incentivize the founder. You started the company owning your shares and then investors come in and want you to start over again (or at least some percentage of it again). It's my company, you say, you want me to re-earn the right to own my piece of my company? The VC is simply trying to make sure that you remain committed to the "mission." They are about to give you gobs of money, after all. One way to have a strong bargaining position is by setting up a vesting schedule from Day 1. It's much rarer that the investor will ask you to reset that clock. Or let's say you owned your shares outright from the start. It's fine to agree to maybe re-vest 25% over one year, or even better, keep everything you've already vested and instead demand an option top-up. You're being diluted and continuing to work, so why shouldn't you get re-upped too, just like the option pool? Another point or two, vested ratably across four years, with a one year cliff, is a great win. Then ask for this on *every single round*.

Investors will also declare that a round will require an option pool top-up. The new investor will claim they want this to be large enough so that you don't run out of options between rounds but the real reason is this: They really don't want you to create too few options and then have to dilute *them* before the next round and certainly as little as possible on the next round. VCs will ask for a 10.0% or 12.5% unallocated option pool post-closing, sometimes without asking you about hiring plans or even the current number of outstanding options. I've even seen paper go as far as 15.0%. Founders should want the pool to be just big enough to hire people until the next round, because on the first round of funding, it's dilutive to founders and *only founders*. If the term sheet asks for a 12.5% option pool, but your hiring plans call for only 5.0% of the total cap table to be issued, then there's 7.5 points of padding. You can increase it again in the next round, when it's dilutive to all shareholders.

I personally tend to go as small as possible. If you can get this down to 7.5%, you're outstanding. This is terrible of me to say. "But don't you want to compensate employees a ton?" Yes, I do. If you do the math and actually assign estimated share counts to all the employees you'll be hiring before the next round, you'll explicitly see the over-padding or that most companies overcompensate equity because they believe that's what market is.

There are a number of terms that will require preferred approval. These may include things like thresholds for an exit, fundraises, debt, the maximum contract size or option grant you can sign without notification, whether you have the right to vote your shares in key moments if you're not still working for the company (the dreaded "then providing services" clause), and so on. Fight as hard as you can to make these as small or nonexistent as you possibly can. Some of these are awful (if you're a shareholder, you're a shareholder and your employment status shouldn't matter), and some are purely operational (if you have to get approval for every contract, you operate slowly). And they may not matter today, but know that they can and will impact your ability to run quickly and avoid arguments with unreasonable board members.

Now for legal fees. This is a dumb term and I couldn't disagree with my co-author more. You are giving me millions of dollars and you want to ask me to pay for your legal fees? *You* pay for your legal fees. I pay for mine and you pay for yours. In later rounds, the founder *doesn't* pay for all the ancillary investors' fees—only the lead's—so the logic that you're covering everyone's is silly. Investors do a hundred deals across the lifetime of the fund; they can put aside some money for legal or cut a deal with their law firm. They do this with carry and other **fund expenses**; why not with raises? It's a cost of doing business. Carve this back hard. The maximum I've ever paid is $25,000, the minimum $0, and the average $10,000. This is probably the most productive thing to do because it fits right into the argument of simply updating the prior round's docs. "I expect us to take the last round's docs, update the numbers, and send them over. I don't foresee any big changes from those, so I think [$5,000] should be plenty." Or just take this logic and throw it right back in their face and say, "Okay! We're raising $10 million so why don't you wire me $10,010,000 instead for the same price?"

Now, I've saved control for last but it's the most important thing. If you are in control, your future is yours; if you're not, it's not. It's that simple. It's also not that simple because there are many forms of control and they must each be individually and wholly considered. There's legal control and tacit control and manipulation and guilt and all sorts of forms of control.

Let's start with board control. The keys to winning will depend on the total number, who holds what seat, and who appoints what seat.

Boards are typically formulated in odd numbers: three, five, seven; larger companies may go nine-plus.

I find it helpful to pose questions as I think about the right type of board for my company. It grounds the theoretical into actual situations:

- Is it clear what type of stock controls the total vote count?
- What does it take to fire you, the founder CEO?
- What does it take to fire a non-founder CEO?
- What does it take to remove all the co-founders?
- What can or can't you do, per the Investor Rights Agreement (e.g., acquisitions rejected under a certain threshold)?

Let's examine some real-world language:

Scenario 1: "The Board shall be comprised of one Preferred seat and two Common seats."

Translation: You'll typically see this in early stages. Founders outvote investors in this scenario. The founder CEO will be on the board, although it isn't specified. If there's one founder, the third seat will typically be vacant. If there are three or more founders, then typically two of them (the CEO and one other) will sit on the board. This is a founder-friendly composition.

Scenario 2: "The Board shall be comprised of two Preferred seats and three Common seats, of which one will be the CEO."

Translation: While technically founders outvote investors, the moment the founder CEO is replaced, founders have lost control even though the seats are specified as common. Why is that? Because the CEO can vote with whomever they want, and if they're a hired gun they'll vote with investors. You could argue that the common seats could fire the CEO ("majority of the Common" appoints the seats, meaning the founders) and then appoint a new one, but it's likely major investors will have a say over that appointment through other rights. It's also, of course, not practical to think about firing the CEO every time you don't like something they're doing or there's a major vote coming up, so generally if a founder isn't CEO the common is pretty much fucked.

Additionally, the language also introduces a way for founders to vote against one another if you are a three-person founding team (two Common team up with one Preferred). As a twosome (and solo) founder, this doesn't come into play because there's no way to get a common majority without both founders.

Scenario 3: "The board shall be comprised of two Preferred seats, two Common seats, and one Independent, which will

be appointed by [1) the majority of the Common / 2) someone mutually agreeable to the majority of the Common and majority of the Preferred].”

Translation: Founders don’t control the board.

This brings up the concept of independent board members. What a gorgeous word chosen to describe such a phantasmic thing! VCs will tell you that Independents are exactly that, not beholden to anyone. They’ll then proceed to introduce you to their buddies or former operators or CEOs or “the” influential person in your space. Be immediately skeptical. They don’t care about anything except this person voting with them, on *every single vote*. The Independent is an investor’s insurance policy for control. If you’re a multi-time founder, it’s possible you do know someone who will be both sufficiently good enough to join the board and *not* be beholden to your investors. Because this seat is the key to control, they’ve got to be someone you truly trust. It’s truly a rarity.

Going back to the legalese: In the first option above, the Common appoints the Independent. It doesn’t matter; you’ve already lost control, and it’s made worse if the CEO isn’t a founder. That’s four against one.

In the second option, it’s even more dire. The Common and Preferred have to agree on the Independent. *Of course* investors will never let you put an Independent on that they don’t like. In this latter scenario, it’s guaranteed you can’t do what you want.

I recently heard that an experienced CEO of a later-stage company negotiates another Common board seat on virtually every fundraise. He never fills those seats, just aggregates seats that he then gets to vote for himself. So even something like an additional board seat can be introduced by founders as part of the negotiation.

In any case, it's also important to remember that just because founders control the board, that doesn't mean they can outvote investors in various scenarios. That would be a mistake. In each round of funding, investor rights agreements exist to ensure that investors safeguard their investment even further. Investors can block financings, acquisitions, term sheets, even key hires that they may disagree with by not approving stock option grants (devious, but it works). For example, the founders might want to take one term sheet over another, but if one of your investors prefers to work with a specific fund or doesn't like the fact that you are taking money off the table, *beware*. Learn the voting thresholds that exist and commit them to memory.

Common Stock and Founder Strife

There's another thing to consider: your co-founder(s). You may not be fighting with them now, but you will. Trust me, you will. People change and priorities change and you'll become misaligned. Voting thresholds will involve the majority of the common and majority means just that. If you are three founders, a majority is two against one. If you are two founders, you may be in a standoff because of the 50% split. Think through a fight and consider this one immutable fact: You are better together than apart. Always. Investors will use any excuse to divide and conquer, and there's no better one than a fight.

Alternatives to the Standard Preferred Majority and How to Ease Strife

As I've gone through more and more financings, I've developed ideas on how I might do things differently the next time. There are alternatives to the "standard" way; consider them as you think through what's right for your company.

Most documents are written as "majority of the preferred" typically for each series. This means that you need to get the approval of the majority of investors for each class of preferred stock every time you want to do something big (like fundraise). It's usually easy to do because there's typically one lead and the rest are smaller checks, but sometimes there isn't just one fund that compromises the majority.

I prefer it when it's less clean, when there's not one controlling investor. It means that you can leverage relationships with earlier, smaller investors to your advantage in moments when you want to do something that the lead investor doesn't.

One alternative focuses on making things difficult. Is it possible to block investors from organizing by making it harder? To accomplish this, perhaps we reject the traditional lead and instead create a syndicate of folks such that the investor who's incensed or on a power trip would need to put in a lot of effort to marshal the votes. You could use **AngelList** to put this into practice or architect it yourself.

Another idea is to decouple investments from seats (discussed further in the next chapter). Perhaps you start the company with language that mandates only one preferred representative for *all* investors. Or perhaps you're the 1% founder (not me) and you minimize investor ownership altogether via super majority shares or having them purchase **common stock**. Then again, if you've earned the leverage to do that, you're probably not reading this book.

Sometimes giving rights to everyone vs. a select few can be helpful. What if notification of changes were a right for all investors? If every investor were notified when there was *any* type of change to a document or cap table, then in times of power struggles the founder CEO might be able to get enough *are you fucking kidding me* from other investors to at least slow down the issue.

You could also consider offering pro rata rights to all investors for every round in perpetuity, or perhaps implement a "use it or lose it" right. You want to exercise your pro rata? Use all of it or your right cedes forever. I've had at least one lead investor refuse to put in their full pro rata out of pure spite, but then these and other rights stuck around in perpetuity and caused major headaches in financings and elsewhere.

Finally, and this is way outside the lines, founders could use employees to stop attacks or create more control. What if any common stock or option holder *must* be notified in the same way as all other major investors? Or perhaps an employee representative is allowed to sit in on all board meetings? Imagine a scenario in which the founder CEO is getting overthrown by co-founders or a power-tripping board member and the entire company had to be notified of exactly what was happening and why. Perhaps a jury of peers is organized, led entirely by a few representatives appointed by the employees, to adjudicate what would happen. As CEO, I'd take those odds any day. Publicity is a deterrent to bad behavior.

(Note: The more I sit on this idea, the more I love it. What a powerful recruiting tool: "You know as much as our investors—full information for all.")

Net: If there is one thing to take away regarding terms and thinking through future political situations, you *must* consider the mechanics of who is sitting where.

Employment Agreements Are a Founder's Friend

One document you also *must* demand if you don't have one: an Employment Contract. It's still at-will employment but this form outlines the scenarios under which you can and cannot be fired, or quit, with or without **Good Reason** or **Cause**. As a founder, especially as founder CEO, and *definitely* if the common isn't in total control of the board, this is key. It can cover severance, COBRA, acceleration of vesting for both founder stock and any options (**single or double trigger**), your ability to keep your board seat, reimbursement for legal fees in the case of wrongful termination, or anything else you deem important to ask for. This agreement may save your financial future in the case of a nasty breakup with your VCs or your co-founders. There's no reason not to have it. Run far, far away from any investor who tells you otherwise.

Now, if founders have to conduct themselves a certain way, why not investors? None of us are immune to bad deeds. You have and will read about some nasty deeds in this book, but it still excludes *really bad behavior* that you hear about in the news, like massive fraud or rape or attempted murder or racketeering. So why don't we all sign morality clauses? Why don't board members sign codes of conduct? We all agree to behave in a specific way—in the way we verbally profess to—now codified in legalese. We deviate from that behavior, and the board has the ability to fire us (as founder, as board member, as VC with the ability to invest in the future).

I've won this in spirit in the past but had the rights carved back to be limited only to conviction vs. including accusation as well. Imagine that: A VC gets handcuffed for allegedly beating their spouse and believes they should retain the right to the board seat. In this instance, they cling to power instead of doing *what their board seat requires of them, which is operating in the company's best interest*. I can't imagine a company in which it is actually helpful to be associated with an abuser; can you? And I can't imagine a founder who wouldn't sign this . . . interesting the self-righteousness that appears here from the capital side.

One final note: The earlier you set the standard for all of these terms, the easier it is to carry into subsequent rounds. For every company I've had, the first set of docs was the basis for every round. It's *really* easy to take your Seed docs, copy paste and update with share counts, and send onto the Series A lead. Later-stage investors will look silly railing against a term an earlier-stage investor was fine with. Set that fair (to you) standard early and later rounds will fall into line.

INVESTOR VIEW: FROM TERM SHEET TO CONTRACT

If the term sheet was standard enough, your lawyer *should* be able to pull contracts off their hard drive and just fill in the blanks, saving everyone a lot of time, money, and stress. But this works only if you use lawyers who know what they're doing and who have done it before. Try to convince the founders to use knowledgeable lawyers as well. Inexperienced lawyers just slow everything down and piss everyone off.

USE EXPERIENCED STARTUP LAWYERS

Years ago I was working on an investment and the startup's lawyer kept asking for nonstandard things. In frustration I asked him how many VC deals he had worked on. "A number of them!" he said, angrily. I looked him up on his firm's website: He had spent his single year since graduating law school working on cattle deals. (This isn't some arcane VC jargon: He literally wrote contracts whose subject was buying and selling cows.) To be fair to him, zero is technically a number.

I called my lawyer. "We should be able to get pretty good terms, since he's new." My lawyer, who was one of the top deal lawyers in the world according to *The American Lawyer* magazine, sighed and said, "We'll get the exact same terms we would have gotten if he was an experienced lawyer, but it will take three times as long and he'll convince his clients you're trying to screw them." That was exactly what happened. Get a lawyer who knows what they're doing and isn't trying to reinvent the wheel.

Tell your lawyers not to get fancy and do not leave them to their own devices. It's fine if they want to argue with the other side's lawyers about boilerplate. But if they get bored they might try to make the deal "better" for you in some meaningful way. They'll improvise and think they're doing you a favor. But in venture capital you don't make your money on the deal structure, you make your money because the company you invested in becomes huge, so nibbling around the edges isn't valuable. And sometimes the lawyer adds things that contradict what the founder and investor already explicitly agreed to. If these things aren't in the term sheet, the lawyer doesn't know about them. This can cause bad blood between founder and investor. For some mysterious psychological reason, each side thinks their own lawyer's freelancing is just a harmless mistake, but if the other side's lawyer is doing it, it's a sinister conspiracy.

DON'T LET YOUR LAWYER FREELANCE

When I invested in the second round of my co-author's first company, her lawyer added a provision to the contract that would have screwed me and that she had told me wouldn't be there. I felt betrayed and tried to call her but she didn't answer. I called her lawyer, yelled at him for five minutes, and hung up. Liz called me back about thirty seconds later. She whispered that the lawyer had overstepped and that I shouldn't worry, she keeps her word. I asked why she was whispering, and she told me she was at a **shiva**. Not my finest moment.

While the docs are getting written and rewritten, something that always seems to take far longer than it should, you're doing deeper due diligence on the company. Most founders understandably don't want you looking under the hood until they have a signed term sheet. But that means you don't get to see a lot of important information until after you've agreed on terms: customer contracts, employment agreements, leases, board resolutions, etc.

Due diligence is pretty standard and I have a list of what I ask founders to show me. My list is based off of some long-ago list I had from another job and is pretty much identical to the due diligence lists of every other VC. Good founders will already know what will be on it and will have someone on their team pulling the stuff together so the process can go smoothly. It makes sense for startups to put all these documents into one place in anticipation of VCs asking to see them. This is called the data room because in the old days all these documents were put into a room in the company's offices to be perused. Nowadays the data room is digital.

Good diligence processes are boring. You read the company's lease (okay, really your lawyer reads the lease and probably most of these others). You read the company's stock option agreement. You read the company's charter and articles of incorporation. You read the company's board decks. You review all of their financial results since the day they started (you should definitely do this one personally). Usually this is painful, because you realize there are problems you didn't know about, mainly because you didn't ask. But once the term sheet is signed, no one really wants to delay the closing. The founder doesn't because they need the money and the investor doesn't because the company needs the money and the longer they wait to give it to them, the worse off the company will be when the deal finally closes. Unless there are some real surprises, you have to swallow your pain and move on. Next time, ask better questions before you issue a term sheet.

When there are surprises and they materially change the value of the business, it's a problem. This is unusual. Founders aren't stupid: They don't usually sign weird leases, they don't usually implement nonstandard option agreements, they usually deal with problems that arise in board meetings, they don't usually lie about things when they know you'll learn the truth before you wire the money. Of course, all these things have turned up in due diligence for one company or another in my years of investing, but they're still the exception, not the rule. Doesn't mean you don't have to do the work.

When there is something surprising, the founder knew that it would be surprising. If they didn't raise it with the investor before due diligence, it's perfectly fair to feel misled. Even to the point of feeling like you either need to change the terms of the deal, or walk away.

FOUNDER VIEW: MANEUVER SKILLFULLY TO THE CLOSE

Sometimes it's okay for a founder to walk away and turn down a term sheet. It's okay to say no to the bird in the hand. It might not be right. It might be too high a valuation. There may be something about the lead that is bothering you, even something you can't put your finger on. You may get something negative when you back channel the firm. The terms might make you queasy. It's *okay to say no*. Founders forget they have power. I've forgotten that at times. You are in control even if it doesn't feel like it.

For the most part, though, deals will close. It's in everyone's best interest. The term sheet turns into long-form docs like the IRA and the SPA and some MRLs. If you've done the term sheet correctly, docs should be seamless. Ask for the most founder-friendly docs from the beginning, and that will set the standard for every raise. Let your lawyers do the hard work for you, and engage with the partner if and only if there is a sticking point. I've experienced "well-intentioned" lawyers on the investor side try to renegotiate percentage ownership changes a few days before a close; it was cleared up in ten seconds by getting on the phone with the partner. Use your lawyers and put as much filth and bickering onto them. You stay shiny and clean and upbeat and get involved only if you're called to.

As you're working toward a close, the investor's attention might wander. Set a close date together and stick to it. It should be no more than four weeks out and ideally three. Time kills all deals. Truly. Email non-leads and keep them up-to-date on docs status. Be a diligent founder and stay present and in touch.

Now, if you've herded the cats properly, the close should be easy. Never close on a Monday (folks are too busy) nor a Friday (folks are checked out). Tuesday, Wednesday, and Thursday are ideal because people are most likely in front of their computer, paying attention.

Know that a close can be hard to do in a single day and that's okay. You need wires to hit in one day (rarely happens) and then the signatures you've collected previously are released from **escrow**. Your investors will have to coordinate internally with **capital calls** and wires being sent. I've had closes happen a day late because a VC wired in time PST but missed the EST deadline at my bank. You actually need to take time zones into account.

Now, if your lead has signed and wired, you're probably good to call it. Let me add one thing that has happened on *every fundraise ever* (no exaggeration): At least one investor does not read instructions and will wire you more or less than they should. Instead of wiring $499,993.42, they will wire $500,000. And you will write them a check back for the $6.58 that you will then hound them to deposit. I'm not kidding. It happens on every round I've ever done. Like . . . did you get rich by not reading instructions? (Actually, yes, you probably did.)

Your lawyers will also need to file a **Form D** with the SEC once the raise is over, on your behalf. It's possible to delay this two weeks without a fine, and longer with one (the fine is tiny). Instruct your lawyers to hold off on the filing until you are ready to announce the round publicly. You'd think these things wouldn't be correlated, but they are. Crunchbase and other websites crawl SEC filings and will list the raise immediately.

This is critical to avoid because publicity is key and also hard to do right. Don't let a bot announce your round for you. A capital raise is a good data point and one that can be press-worthy (although there are so many rounds these days and at such high numbers that it most likely isn't), but if you can join it with another piece of news (e.g., a sexy customer quote), that will make the narrative even more powerful. Plan your timeline carefully.

Know that your investors don't care about your timing desires! They want to announce and move on. They want to tweet! They want to post on LinkedIn! If it's a massive deal, they want to brag at their weekend VC hundred-mile bike excursion. (You're not legally allowed to be a VC unless you participate in an expensive and/or fringe sport. Go search for "Ride and Tie" if you don't believe me.) Tell them to close their mouths and remind them every day until the announcement. In bold letters in email. I've had investors leak the news inadvertently, primarily because they didn't read email. It happens. But you should try to make it happen on your terms.

Lawyers, Architecting a Deal, and QA

No deal is going to get done, and get done well, without three things: a fantastic legal team, an instinct for negotiation, and your time and attention to QA.

First, lawyers. You may think that your lawyers are fantastic and that they'll take care of it for you, but if you are using one of the six law firms that claim to have a competency in startups, you're already in a bad spot. (If you're in doubt as to whether you're working with one of these firms, ask your investors or send me an email.) Investors will tell you that these firms have a ton of experience in startups and are tops. That's true. But they're also beholden to investors because they do hundreds of deals a year for investors and maybe one deal every other year for you. With whom do you think their loyalty lies? Not you. Furthermore, they often work for both sides at the same time; I've personally been in a deal with one firm that was working for three separate parties simultaneously. In any other scenario, lawyers will recuse themselves; not in startupland. They make more money with investors than you and there's no way to change it.

MAKE SURE YOUR LAWYERS WORK FOR YOU

I learned this lesson of contrasts during the Pre-Seed round of my last company. At my first startup, I used one of the Top Six. I thought they were fantastic but the work turned out to be lackluster and it caused me grief when exiting from the acquirer. At my last company, we went with one of the world's top litigation firms. They were absolute pit bulls, as top litigators are, and when we directed them to "make the most founder-friendly docs," they actually did. **NVCA** docs are *not* founder friendly, in case you are wondering. Our docs were so damn friendly, in fact, that they removed anti-dilution provisions (highly standard, highly fair) for investors. My co-author, an investor in that round, was the only one who caught it and signed only because I swore in blood we wouldn't screw him over. (If you are looking for an example of investor/founder trust to the max, ours is it.) You best believe the next round had those provisions included.

A founder recently called me for advice in closing a round. She had hired one of the Top Six. The partner was an incredibly competent lawyer—I was impressed at her ability to perceive strategy and her knowledge of what was and was not possible—but when I went to speak to her on the founder's behalf, she said, "Yes, well, I can push back but I know [FUND_NAME] won't agree to that and so why would we ask for it?" A lawyer's job is to work on behalf of their customer, and in this case, we started from a place that was pro-investor. A negotiation occurs along a spectrum; starting halfway means the founder loses. Net: Find any other competent firm that isn't in bed with the VCs and be done with it.

NO, REALLY, MAKE SURE YOUR LAWYERS WORK FOR YOU

Case in point: My same pit bull lawyers, during the same round of funding, were in the process of collecting signature blocks from investors. They received one that ended with the phrase "by and on behalf of various entities." The lawyers believed this could be interpreted to mean that the fund, once it became a shareholder, could transfer their securities to any other entity they owned. Our lawyer was rightfully concerned that the company would have no power nor control over any such transfers; what if shares were transferred to a competitor, for example?

Our lawyer wrote back and asked for a different signature block. Their partner wrote back and said, "This signature block has been in hundreds of deals around the world and it's not going to change." Our lawyer wrote back to *that*, starting the email with the snarky "Glad to hear your signature block is so well-traveled." You can imagine how it ended.

Unbeknownst to our counsel, the partner he was emailing with was married to a very famous CEO. You *don't* tell this person off.

I had been out playing chess in Central Park in a desperate bid to take an hour off from the fundraise and had left my Blackberry in my apartment. When I got back, I saw that last email and gasped out loud. I called the investor and said the signature block was fine, and then called off the pit bull.

It's dumb and not market and what do you think you're doing?!" then I'm fairly certain I'm not going to have an analytical mind on the other side of the table. Now, if that same person says, "Liz, this is a standard policy designed to protect both you and me. Every private and public company has it, just like New York State has mandatory liability coverage for car insurance. Have you ever bought D&O before? Would it be helpful for me to explain it to you?" then I have a pretty good feeling that this person will most likely start by trying to understand my question instead of immediately reacting.

Another tactic here is grounding the theoretical legalese into concrete situations. Let the lawyers bicker about words like *reasonable*; the high-level business points are going to get ironed out between you and the partner. If we take that bloated option pool example, it's a simple next step to say, "Hey, here is who we're bringing on board, can you help me understand why we need 2.5 times what we'll be allocating to employees?" They'll stammer and you'll get the pool carved down to half the number proposed.

A combination of good lawyers, scheming co-founders, and advisors who have been through this before should be able to help you map out a cogent argument for each term, and certainly the fundraise as a whole. If you get even half of what you're looking for *and* find out who your new board member really is in the process, you've done a fantastic job.

INVESTOR VIEW: TREAT THE FOUNDER FAIRLY NOW OR IT WILL COME BACK TO BITE YOU LATER

I enjoy talking with founders and trying to get to a point where I can back them. I enjoy working with them after the investment, helping them think through building their companies. But getting from term sheet to signed contract is a grind.

There are only two kinds of terms in an investor's term sheet: the nonnegotiable and the irrelevant. Okay, that's an exaggeration. Everything is a little bit negotiable, but if the founder counters an offer with a wildly different valuation or a lopsided board composition, disciplined investors will bend but not break. And if the founder tries to negotiate most of the other terms, the investor will (hopefully) calmly explain why those terms are much more important for them than they are detrimental to the founder. This is usually even true.

That said, I think every investor who has never raised money from a VC has to understand that it's not just work to a founder, it's survival. The period between getting the term sheet and signing the contract is the moment when the biggest power imbalance in the entire relationship exists. That's probably why, to me, an investor, it's just work, while to a previous me, a founder, it was terrifying. If the negotiation goes poorly, investors can just stand up and walk away. If the investor walks away, the company may cease to exist.

I remember, as a founder, the feeling of powerlessness as investors and their lawyers demanded pointless but time-consuming clauses in the contract. When they gave me their term sheet, I shut down my search for other investors at their insistence. Then, a month into negotiating the contract, my company was low on cash. We didn't have time to restart the process. We had zero negotiating leverage. When they asked for things that made no sense, it didn't seem like negotiating, it seemed like bullying.

I'm not saying the investor should pity the founder. But you should be aware of how the term sheet/contract negotiation feels to them. You should be aware of the power imbalance. What may seem to you like a jolly debate over co-sale rights may seem to the founder like you trying to crush any chance of them succeeding. A good founder won't be daunted, but they also won't forget.

As the investor, you need to negotiate for terms that make sense, but you have to treat the founder fairly, openly, and honestly. You are going to work with them until the company either IPOs, sells, or fails. How you treat them when you have all the power will determine the tenor of the relationship for those next ten years.

FOUNDER VIEW: TAKE 'EM TO SCHOOL

Everything I've written in this chapter may not be possible for you and your co-founders to get. But knowing what other opportunities exist outside of the "standard"—and I'm sure other things are possible far beyond this—is worst case information and best case life changing.

On the flip side, if you get everything you want, it also doesn't mean unexpected or bad things won't happen to you (they certainly did to me). *That doesn't mean you shouldn't try.*

It's also important to caveat everything I've written by acknowledging that I'm not a normal founder. I'm not the best but I'm more than two standard deviations above the mean. I have pushed the boundaries of what is possible in fundraises, in documents, in board meetings, and in running a company in general. I've raised from the top names and had those same names on my Board.

My success has been made possible for the following reasons:

1. **I'm very good at getting people to like me quickly.** I can't tell you why, so I asked four folks (two who worked for me, one customer, one investor) to do it for me. Their take:

    - She communicates with a level of genuine authenticity.
    - She means precisely what she says.

- For those who prefer the straightforward approach, Liz is a refreshing and fantastic partner.
- She immediately treats you like an old friend. No stuffy formality or cautious reserve.

It's not all roses, of course. One of my co-founders once said to me that the things that make us great are also the reasons why people dislike us. I'm no exception.

But once someone likes me, it's all fair game. Some years ago, another of my co-founders noticed that I seemed to be able to get any investor to laugh at anything I said. He dared me to see how far I could push it. At the next opportunity, I lifted up my foot to essentially shove a filthy Vans slip-on covered in shark pattern into a VC's face. He laughed. The coup de grace, though, was pitching an investor group over Zoom, holding up a can of Diet Coke only a few minutes in, and giggling; they laughed right back. It was insane. This ability became a pillar for successful fundraising and sales.

2. **I've been surrounded by co-founders whose brains are the size of planets.** Lots of people have said lots of things, negative and positive, about each of my three co-founders. Lots of people have said lots of things about me too. Some of the negatives turned out to be spot-on, for each of us. But, man . . . each of my co-founders could really think, and in ways I couldn't or wasn't good at or didn't even know existed. Good founding teams are Venn diagrams and the smaller the overlap, the better. Just make sure you actually like each other.

3. **I've had help.** I've been lucky enough to have been part of a team that most recently built and sold the best product in the top company in a white-hot space. Right place, right time,

right product. I've also been lucky enough to have people who care deeply about me and my company's success, who are willing to help at all hours of the day and night. There are moments where I've felt so grateful I've cried.

4. **I've got giant balls.** I get irritated when people talk about all the ways in which things aren't possible, could go wrong, and are hard. Yes. There are myriad ways in which things could fail. It doesn't matter if we're talking about hanging a picture or buying a second home or testing a product feature. There are also myriad ways that things could go right. I (at least professionally) like to say, "What's the best thing that could happen?" I've said it so many times to friends and family that when faced with a recent difficult decision, my brother reminded *me* that everything was an implementation detail in the end.

   I've done pretty ballsy things and also had a solid instinct on when to do and not do them. I pretended I met a bigshot at a conference in order to get their attention and money (successfully, I might add). I've fudged where I've lived in order to get funding. I convinced a successful exited founder to get off the couch and join my company. You never, EVER know until you try. So try. The worst that can happen is someone says no.

5. **I like to win.** The better I've gotten at the game, the more I want to play it. It's actually the only game where that's the case. I typically get decent at things and then lose interest. Not this game.

   You and your co-founders may have some, all, or none of the above characteristics. You may have others or even more. No matter what, these terms are the next ten years of your life. Try as hard as you can to get as much as you can without jeopardizing the deal, because operating in good faith, being a good person, and working hard does not necessarily protect you. Trust me when I say your financial and company's future depend on it.

KEY TAKEAWAYS

FOUNDER	INVESTOR
Don't rush to sign. It's overwhelming but a mistake. Read the term sheet thoroughly and think through its implications carefully.	Terms and contracts ensure both sides know exactly what they have agreed to; it should never get to the point where one side has to sue to enforce them.
Know what's possible even if you can't get it. Information is power.	Founders and investors must talk to many people to know what prevailing investment terms are.
It's okay to walk away and say no. That might even get you what you want.	A bad deal up front will come back to haunt the relationship later.
VCs have been known to blow up deals. If it happens to you, you will survive.	Good VCs do what they say they are going to do. VCs should only pull a term sheet if they were misled by the founder.
The "right" term sheet is nuanced. Price is not everything. Control *is* everything. Negotiating is an art.	Founders choose term sheets based on valuation but other terms matter just as much. Don't minimize their importance.
Lawyers are in bed with VCs. Find ones who aren't.	Use lawyers who know what they are doing. It will be cheaper and easier.
If the founding team isn't perfectly aligned, control will be lost.	How a VC treats a founder during this process sets the stage for the rest of the relationship.

4

THE BOARD OF DIRECTORS

INVESTOR VIEW: WHY STARTUPS HAVE A BOARD

Most entrepreneurs start companies because they don't want to work for someone else. Those who raise venture capital find they once again have a boss: their board of directors.

In theory, corporations are owned by their shareholders. In practice, this is a bit tenuous. I own some shares of Amazon, but if I tried to walk into their headquarters uninvited I don't think the security guards would be swayed by me insisting that I own the place. But as an Amazon shareholder I get to help make some decisions about how the place is run. I get to vote for who is on the board of directors. In turn, these directors are the people who get to run the company. They usually do this by delegating running the company to the CEO. But they retain the power to intervene, either by taking back some of the CEO's responsibilities or by replacing the CEO. The basic principle is the same in a venture-backed company: Shareholders elect board members who run the company, primarily by delegating to the CEO.

Venture capitalists invest in people they think can run a company, but they elect themselves to seats on the board to cover their bases. VCs hope board meetings keep them apprised of how the company is doing, its plans for the near future, any problems it is facing, and what it is doing about them. They want to know how their money is being used, and if their investment remains a worthwhile one.

CEOs often seem to misunderstand what the board is for. If they are optimists, they think it is a gathering of advisors, there to help them manage the company. If they are pessimists, they think its sole purpose is to make their life hell. Many founders seem to believe both of these things at once.

I've known board members who were indispensable advisors and board members who were complete idiots, but both of these things were incidental to them being on the board. The board is not about the people, it is about the job it is meant to do: provide oversight of the company. If managed correctly, this job helps the company succeed.

If managed incorrectly, board meetings can be uniquely dangerous breeding grounds for founder-investor disputes. A mismanaged board meeting can give rise to investor disgruntlement, and that can lead to the board using one of the few tools it has at its disposal when these disputes get out of hand: replacing the CEO.

FOUNDER VIEW: WHY BOARDS CONFLICT FROM DAY ONE

I have been the founder CEO and board member at two companies, and I've presented in front of two other boards of companies at which I've worked. I have cried in more meetings than I can count, had board members who were purposefully cruel, checked email constantly, or didn't say a word about the dynamic live but called me later to vent. I've had one regularly fall asleep. I've had executives present to the board and played that silly role myself. I've lost board control due to investor ego and founder disagreements. I'll pull the conclusion up front: Boards suck and nothing you do matters.

The board of directors is a group of people whose legal and fiduciary obligation is to oversee the company and ensure it serves the best interests of all shareholders. Let me say that again: The board operates on behalf of *all shareholders*. If an investor holds a seat, their job is *not* to protect the returns of their fund. If a founder holds a seat, their job is *not* to hold onto power.

Yeah, right. You can see why problems arise. If an investor's job is to maximize their funds' returns and a founder's job is to put their vision into the world, the company comes second. Conflict abounds.

I asked a Seed stage venture capitalist what he thought about this:

This is a business relationship. I'm signing up to make the business successful. At the early stages, the business is one-to-one with the founders. It's the founders' vision and I need to make them successful to make the business successful.

But sometimes the founders become the barrier, hell-bent on not being successful, because instead of winning they want to be right about some specific thing, or have things their way just because, or have their ego placed above the lives and paychecks of their employees etc., etc. In those situations, if they don't stop being the problem, they're gonna get fired. Helping a founder destroy a company by standing by and doing jack shit in the name of not crossing them does not generate returns.

On the flip side, sometimes the business is just not going to work no matter what anyone does. But you believe in the founders' capacity to figure something out and you support them in finding a business that will work.

Part of being a good VC is knowing what situation you're dealing with and acting accordingly.

Every VC that says they themselves are like founders are lying. They might have been, once upon a time. But roles carry a lot of weight and influence on one's own behavior. Some who say they are founder friendly really are, in the sense that they will literally do nothing other than what the founders want, including standing idly by while a founder burns someone's pension money into the ground. Many aren't founder friendly, but say they are. Most seem to be low-key lackadaisical, as soon as the deal is closed. Some seem to be more hands on, but nuanced about their alignment to the success of the business vs. the founders. "

This investor raises great points. He believes that his job *is* safeguarding the shareholders' interests (and I know for a fact he does this job well). But he identifies the crux of the problem: Investors back founders who run businesses, and yet founders are fallible and independent of the business, and so what happens when an investor loses faith in a founder's ability to execute? Do they stand idly by? Fire them? Do something in the middle?

INVESTOR VIEW: VENTURE-BACKED BOARDS ARE DIFFERENT

The standard view is that the members of the board of directors are (1) the big bosses who show up at a company to (2) listen to, and sometimes argue with, the CEO. They are (3) elected by, and (4) represent the shareholders, the owners of the company. It is their job to (5) hold management to account.

In a venture-backed company the reality is different.

1. **The board is not the boss in any meaningful sense but one.** No founder looks to their board to tell them what to do on a regular basis, and no functional board wants to be the entity managing the company. The board looks to the CEO to manage the company. Board members may offer advice and criticism, but usually—again, if the board is a well-functioning one—only if the board member has some unique insight from previous work or if they feel the CEO is missing something important or not listening to advice. I've used the caveat *functional* twice because not every board functions well, and we'll talk about that in a bit.

2. **Board members do listen to, and they do argue with, the CEO.** But just listening is a failure of leadership by the board, and just arguing is a failure of leadership by the CEO. Board members are in board meetings to learn, which takes more than listening. And they are there to advise, but, frankly, if the advising turns to arguing or

lecturing, it's a process failure. Strong disagreements should not make it as far as a board meeting; they must be addressed earlier.

3. **Board members are not chosen by all the shareholders.** In venture-backed startups, every time a new round of capital is raised, the contracts specify who gets to appoint board directors. The new investor usually gets one or two, the previous investors get one or two, the founders get one or two, and so on. So, while shareholders technically do elect board members, it's a sort of Chinese democracy: You can vote for anyone you want, as long as it's the preapproved candidates.

4. **This leads to some interesting dynamics.** With the caveat (again) that I'm not a lawyer, board members have a duty under the law to make decisions that, in their judgment, are best for all the shareholders. But, as Liz's VC friend said, if you're the board member appointed by a venture capital firm—often the partner who convinced the fund to invest—you have a powerful incentive to do what is best for you and your firm, not necessarily what is best for the company. The founder has a similar conflict: They may want to protect their job and power, and that may influence what they do in board meetings and, ultimately, how they run the company.

Startup boards are usually implicitly adversarial this way. All board members know they are supposed to look out for the best interests of all the shareholders but are also, naturally, concerned with their own interests. They are also aware that other directors are self-interested behind the mask of fiduciary duty. Board meetings can become intensely political, where the links between intentions and decisions are unsaid.

5. **True; the board's job is to hold management to account.** Board oversight of management is distinct from the other things good board members do to make the company successful: They help the founder with the big vision, make sure appropriate policies and controls are in place, and stay on top of the company's progress to make sure the CEO is managing through problems and changing conditions.

Board members, as well-informed outsiders, can also provide advice that isn't strictly "on behalf of all shareholders," but they should be clear which hat they're wearing when they do: The oversight hat? The trusted advisor hat? The friend of the founder hat? The protecting my (and only my) investment hat? When things are going well at a company, all these roles may seem the same, so people muddle them. But it's good practice not to, because when things aren't going well the roles can result in very different advice.

Good board members approach their board seat constructively and are an asset to the company. Some act more defensively, and these investors can cause problems by needing exacting reassurance that things are going fine, or overreacting to snags along the way. The CEO's job in managing the board is recognizing who is who, and figuring out how to deal with each of them.

CEOs usually do not want or expect the board to manage *them*. They often think the board's purpose is entirely different—sometimes this is wishful thinking but usually it is the result of an investor not being entirely forthright during the raise—and are disappointed when it is not. The reality is that while the board can be very helpful, it is always and primarily a check on the CEO's power.

FOUNDER VIEW: THE FUTILITY OF BOARD MEETINGS

Here is what I originally hoped the board could do for me and what investors professed they *did* do:

- Help me think through problems and push back on assumptions.
- Provide intel on market trends, anything competition-related, rumored fundraises, **M&A**.
- Be a nonjudgmental ear.
- Make introductions to prospective customers, executives, and independent board members (and then help sell them in).
- Walk me through case studies of other similar companies to guide me on the types of things I should start thinking about now.
- Be unfailingly supportive.
- Contribute to a meeting that's actually productive.

This doesn't exist. It also can never exist because of the way the entire thing is constructed.

Board members simply aren't operators (even ones who were aren't now, and as Jerry mentions in Exits, those skills have a half-life of only a few years). And so, in setting up for a meeting or a conversation with a board member, you, the founder CEO, will spend a ton of time prepping for . . . what exactly? If you are good at your job, you already know what is bad and what is good. What you *actually* need is a sounding board (no pun intended) to think through the big problems. Say your number one problem is that your team is having difficulty converting a first demo to a second meeting. It's simply not helpful for your board to tell you that you're not hitting revenue targets. *Of course you're not hitting your revenue targets*. You, the founder CEO, just proactively declared that and asked for help with *the* issue in your funnel.

Instead, each board meeting will descend into a tedious, often abusive session in which the investors tell you what a bad job you're doing. I was once pushed so far that I called an investor an asshole to his face, to which he said, "Yes I am, but I'm preparing you for the even bigger ones." This same investor later ranted over the phone about his tanked NPS score, saying that he "had the highest one of anyone at the firm for years" and that I had ruined it on purpose and refused to admit it to him, to which I said, "You're damn straight it was me. I gave you zeros across the fucking board." So yes, in case you are wondering, there actually is no bigger asshole than this man.

These types of interactions are simply not helpful. Founders need construction, not destruction. And you spend time preparing for this unhelpful hour, and I pity you if your hour is in fact two or ten. The most absurd part about the time you spend preparing is that you spend *insane* amounts of time preparing, like *days*. It once got to the point that I refused to allocate more than a few hours on the weekend to pulling together a deck that nobody would read ahead of time. My co-founder and I would stare at each other balefully, shaking our heads that even this small part of our weekend was wasted on such drivel.

My co-author disagrees with this perspective. He'll say that if you're tracking key metrics already, it should be easy to pull together a deck and fairly simple to clue in board members before the meeting such that there are no surprises. He believes it should be fairly painless to show folks you're doing a good job.

The challenge is that each board deck must be a work of art because it has to address all the ego and opinions in the room. It requires intensely careful crafting so as to spotlight what *I* want people to pay attention to and distract them from what I don't. The scope of preparing for a board meeting—the deck, objection handling with your co-founders, the orchestration of who says what when, the phone calls reviewing the information beforehand with each VC individually—is so burdensome that I think of the effort as akin to mini-fundraises. Jerry will later call it a pageant and I couldn't agree more.

The effort also exists irrespective of how the company is actually doing. If it's going well, investors are going to dig in hard. What am I not seeing? What's around the corner? Why isn't this better or that better? They're going to question the information I present *because* things are going well. If things are going well, then they can be going better.

And if the business is in the shitter, then *every single thing* I present is going to be picked apart, every decision questioned. I'll be asked to walk through each problem in minute detail and will also be required to hold my tongue when it becomes obvious they haven't been paying attention up until now, because most of what they say will be generic self-gratification or clarification on the basics of the business.

The best part is when investor advice changes in a heartbeat, most notably present when markets enter a down period. If you thought their advice was single-minded, flippant, and irrational before, get ready for it in times of contraction. You'll go from "Make sure you have those unit economics locked down and don't you dare spend another dollar on marketing until you do" to "It's a race to number one, why the heck aren't you [HIRING/SCALING/WINNING] more?" Investors care when they decide to care and good luck if they decide to *really* care today.

I've found board meetings to be so onerous that I actively developed ways to waste the investors' time. I embrace Jerry's dog-and-pony show and consistently develop red herring slides just to distract from criticism. I'll invite long-winded executives to present a deck they invested two weeks of their life building to kill time (bonus: the executive feels extra special they were even invited). The truth is that every one of these meetings I've had for the past fifteen years has culminated in such exhaustion that I've learned to take every afternoon off afterward. And my work stamina is outstanding.

I had high hopes, once upon a time. Whenever I bring on a new big investor, I try to give them a PhD in the company. The goal is to ensure they know the business as well as they can so that they can be as helpful as possible. That means going through a product demo, the sales pitch, pipeline, meeting employees, a call or two with a customer, everything. Instead, I'm lucky if I get two hours of their attention.

The last time I did it, the new investor fidgeted for an hour and then said, "Why don't you get a real office? This place is a shithole." Another board member regularly said to me that "I take pride in the fact that I've never seen a demo." It became a running joke for them and mind-boggling for me. You've put money into a company, you sit on the board, you want to help, and you don't want to actually look at the thing? Can't wait for the next board meeting! It will be so helpful.

INVESTOR VIEW: MAKE BOARD MEETINGS PRODUCTIVE

Some investors are arrogant, some of them are afraid, some of them have no social skills, some of them are just plain annoying. This can cause conflict, but that's life. There's a difference, though, between board members being difficult to deal with because of personality conflicts and board members being difficult to deal with because they think the business isn't going in the right direction or the founder isn't paying attention to the right things.

A company's VCs invested in more than a founder; they invested in a vision. The investors on a board of directors help keep founders on plan. And founders need this, to one extent or another. Engineer-founders can fall prey to building the coolest product at the expense of building a business. Businessperson-founders tend toward marketing an amazing story at the expense of building an actual product. Neither of these things work on their own; they are both needed. A good board will tell the engineer-founder to ship and will tell the businessperson-founder to build. A good board will abstract out the details and remind the founder to focus on the big picture.

A good board will also focus on the details, if the details are legitimately troubling. When the plan is failing so badly that it's endangering the company then the plan needs to change. If the CEO isn't driving that conversation then the board will think the CEO isn't doing their job.

This situation, from the board members' point of view, usually starts in a board meeting. The CEO is going through their deck and shows a slide with information the board members have never seen before. It might be a lost customer, a missed revenue forecast, a higher-than-expected cash burn, or even something as mundane as a chart of conversion rates over time showing some flattening. The CEO may try to avoid talking about the issue, point out the problem and try to move on, or point out the problem and ask for advice.

In the first two cases, good board members will stop the CEO and ask about the issue. This is oversight. If the CEO doesn't know the details or doesn't have a plan for dealing with the issue, trouble can ensue. In the last case, jump straight to the trouble.

Bad board members—and it's a rare board without any—will jump in. They will either point out the obvious—"This is a real problem!"—or start to spray the CEO with questions. Other board members, not wanting to seem lax in front of their peers, join in.

There's a downward spiral, the issue remains unresolved, the CEO looks weak, and the board members, even the good ones, are left wondering if the CEO is the right person to lead the company.

This is the worst case. But it's not an exaggeration. I've seen this exact situation on at least half the boards I've been on. It has never led directly to a CEO's firing, but it has always contributed to investor discontent, and that discontent has influenced future decisions about the CEO.

In a good board meeting, the CEO presents updates on important issues—key business metrics, progress on building the product, hiring, the customer funnel, customer feedback, the balance sheet or income statement—whatever is important at that stage of the company, and shows how the company is trending compared to goals. They highlight any problems or opportunities and talk about what they are doing to fix problems or take advantage of opportunities. This is the meat of the deck. The CEO then goes deeper on a couple of the biggest problems or opportunities, telling the board about their thought process in addressing them. Last, they talk about the company goals and whether they need to be revised in light of the latest learnings, or if they are still what the company should be aiming for.

There are two really important things in all of this. First, every problem or opportunity comes with a recommended course of action. And second, there are no surprises in the board meeting. I'll say it again: Board meetings are not the right place to solve problems. If the CEO needs help solving a problem, that's fine, but they should get that help well before the meeting.

The CEO should make it easy for board members to keep on top of what is happening. Continuity in presentation lets them keep track, meeting to meeting, of what's happening and how problems are being resolved. By comparing the last meeting's board deck to this meeting's deck, investors can remember decisions made at previous meetings, relieving the board of having to have the same conversations over and over, and see which things are not being talked about. I understand the impulse to delay talking about unsolved problems until they are better understood, but good board members need to stay on top of these. "Mr. Corleone is a man who insists on hearing bad news immediately."

I'm talking about all the things the *CEO* needs to do because the investor sometimes needs to be the one to tell them to do it. If you feel like you're not informed enough to provide proper oversight, tell the CEO what you need. Make sure it's in writing, and make sure they give it to you at the next and subsequent meetings.

CEOs often complain they waste time preparing for board meetings, and it's true that some board members want information they don't need. Don't ask the CEO to waste time, time they could be using to build the company. Some suggestions:

1. Professionalism is one thing—decks should be proofread, etc.—but don't ask for glitz; let them save the glitz for the customer-facing material.

2. Make sure the CEO is focusing on what's important. They might feel like they need to distract you with a dog-and-pony show, trotting senior management out to tell you details of their day-to-day. This is a waste of their time to organize, a waste of senior management's time to prepare for, and a waste of your time to listen to. Yes, you need to know senior management, but sit with them outside the meeting, when it's unscripted.

3. Help the CEO make good decisions about what is important to present, and revise these as the company grows. Do this outside of formal board meetings. It requires some real thought and insight, and decision-making as a group is the least efficient process known to mankind.

4. If collecting data to show how the company is doing is time-consuming for the team, either the board is asking for things that aren't important or the company isn't habitually monitoring the important things. Which is it?

It can take time for the CEO to put everything on paper in a way that board members can digest, and that's unavoidable. But keep in mind that, as an investor, you're the one paying for wasted time. Minimize it by being mindful of what you and other board members ask for.

Review the deck ahead of time, look for issues, and discuss them with the CEO before you get to the meeting. This means you need to see the board deck earlier than the night before the meeting and then reserve time to review it immediately upon receiving it. Many board members won't, which makes it even more important that you do. If the issues are big ones, you should advise the CEO to discuss them with all the board members beforehand. Surprises lead to chaotic meetings, and that's just a waste of everybody's time.

If I'm close with the CEO, they often ask me to review the board deck even before the rest of the board sees it. That way I can help clarify the deck and point out things that might cause issues for other board members.

If there are no surprises, and everyone is prepared, the board meetings will run smoothly and go quickly. In general, having board meetings of two hours or less every other month (for an early-stage company) is better than longer meetings (there shouldn't be *that* much to talk about, if there are no surprises) or meetings further apart (the board members will forget everything about the company if they're not updated regularly).

After the meeting, call the CEO and tell them how you thought it went. Tell them if you think the presentation should be revised, if other company executives should be there, how the other board members reacted to it all, and so on. Be constructive, but make sure they get the feedback. Get feedback from the CEO also. Was the discussion helpful? Were some board members not doing their job? You can help solve these problems outside the boardroom. Do your job as a board member—once again: oversight—but don't let it get in the way of the CEO doing their job.

FOUNDER VIEW: MAKE BOARD MEETINGS SUCK LESS

I believe the only point of a board meeting is to get things approved, like option grants or compensation adjustments. That's it. Your board may have other ideas, though, and it will be hard to not go along with those ideas. The sad truth is that we all profess to be in these meetings for governance and accountability purposes, and yet my experience is that these never seem to be the primary driver of conversation.

I shared a stage with my co-author recently and told the audience that I'd rather not have a board at all. An audience member called me out by asking, "Why would I want to invest in someone who doesn't want to be held accountable?" It's a fair point; trust, but verify, right? My co-author responded that my desire to not have a board didn't mean that I wasn't accountable, and that if I was anything, it was accountable.

I suppose what I'm looking for is a fresh approach to the board, and we'll talk shortly about how I create one that's useful for me (my true board, as it were), but in the meantime, boards as they exist today are what they are and neither I nor this book is going to change that. So what can you, the founder CEO, do to ensure you get value (cue vomiting) from these people and interactions? Let's approach it from a perspective of "How good could I make it?" vs. "How can I prevent it from being so bad?"

First, try to make these meetings as infrequent and short as possible. When you're negotiating the long-form docs (the term sheet will typically be silent on this point), you'll have a list of things you care about strongly enough such that you will push back, and hard. If your investors choose to write frequent board meetings into the bylaws, *this* is one I fight for. Why would I sign my name to a document that legally binds me to prepare and show up for meetings that are wasteful? I wouldn't. If you can get these to once a quarter and no more than ninety minutes, you're in a good spot.

Next, as with any relationship, those with your board members are strategic and thus require you to architect them as you would any other plan. What do they excel at that you can leverage? How can you make them feel good so that they might actually listen when you call? Is there a way to create a relationship such that they will call you first before talking behind your back? Craft these relationships as carefully as you bicker over the font choice in your Admin UI with your head of product.

Invest in what your VCs do well (some of this was learned in diligence while fundraising). Maybe they can help you close candidates through salesmanship and the mystique of their name, if they're famous (or notorious) enough. Perhaps they can help you think through politics you may have with other investors or regarding a decision. Or they may be wonderful to share a meal with and certainly have connections and favors to bestow upon you should they like you. Find this competency and learn to extract everything you can from it.

There's also the board meeting itself. Early on, a successful late-stage founder told me that nothing should happen in board meetings that I didn't expect. Decisions, discussion, objections—all this should be a fait accompli because I prepped by having a pre-board board meeting with each member one-on-one. I laughed and told him that was an even worse waste of time than the meetings themselves and proceeded to ignore him. Then I raised more money and the stakes became more complicated, and I would desperately invite other prominent folks as a way to strategically mitigate the various egos that existed. After only one meeting post-raise, I decided that founder was right. Prep calls also mean the investor gets to replay their suggestions *in the board meeting itself*, which also makes the investor (1) feel useful and (2) look good in front of other investors. Making investors look good in front of other investors is *very* important.

While board meetings themselves are a waste of time and you waste time preparing for that waste of time, what isn't a waste of time is investing in the relationships. While this technically isn't board prep, I spend regular time updating my investors, having them help me "think through problems" or "get their advice." Like the "picking a fight" negotiation suggestion in the Terms chapter, this is a way to manage up so that investors think you are coachable and listen. The more time you spend with investors, the fonder they become of you. In a horrific scenario in which you are getting fired, it's possible that investor guilt becomes your tool of last resort.

Board members, and I suppose investors in general, fall into two categories: harmful or helpful. If you own a piece of my company, you better be sure to do *something, anything* to make it more valuable.

Invest time in trying to make these meetings suck a little bit less. Even a slight alleviation of pain is worth it.

INVESTOR VIEW: AVOID ANTAGONIZING THE FOUNDER

Nobody wants to make the company more valuable than the investors do—that may be the only thing they *do* care about. But VCs have to work through the CEO to get things done. Sometimes the best way to do this is by asking probing and, possibly, leading questions; getting hands-on involved is almost never going to do much. Liz has accused me of not always being direct, and this is true. If it's a choice between getting the credit and getting my way, I'll always choose the latter. Sometimes this requires convincing the CEO that the right thing to do was their idea all along. And sometimes it means backing away from a fight before defensiveness hardens into stubbornness.

DON'T GET TUNED OUT

A VC complained to me recently about a CEO who would not take his advice, despite obvious signs that key metrics were trending in the wrong direction. "I called the CEO every week and tried to get him to fix the problem. We had the same conversation over and over, but he never listened. After a while he wouldn't even return my calls," the VC said.

The salient lesson for any investor is that, hard as it is to get a CEO to take your advice, it is impossible when they are no longer willing to talk to you at all. No matter how contentious it gets, you have to keep the lines of communication open. Your ability to have any influence whatsoever depends on it.

Winston Churchill's mother, Jennie Jerome, once had dinner with William Gladstone and Benjamin Disraeli in the same week. "When I left the dining room after sitting next to Gladstone, I thought he was the cleverest man in England. But when I sat next to Disraeli I left feeling that I was the cleverest woman." As an investor, you can get founders to listen to you either by being the smartest person in the room or by making them feel like the smartest. But, frankly, if you're smarter than all the founders you invest in, maybe you need to find more impressive founders. Leading founders to find the right answers themselves takes a soft touch.

If the situation isn't urgent, and the CEO and I disagree on how to handle it, I usually stand aside while the CEO tries their solution. Once it doesn't work, and they realize I had a point, they're much more likely to listen in the future.

This sounds arrogant, but it's not. When I was a young VC I asked a mentor how to get CEOs to listen to my advice. "That's easy," he said, "just always be right." I stewed on this for a long time. How could I always be right? Eventually I decided that what he meant was not to give unequivocal advice except when you're certain. All other times, you don't give advice, you work through the problem with the CEO, arriving at a way forward. This is the opposite of arrogance: When you can't know something, humility is in order. You build trust by being careful about what you do and don't really know.

Even if you and the CEO get along, the board is usually more than just the two of you. It might be five or seven people. Now you have multiple people whose idiosyncrasies can clash.

On top of that, investors have complicated feelings about each other. The VC world is relatively small, and it's intensely interconnected. VCs need to know other VCs: Early-stage VCs need to know later-stage VCs so they can get them to look at their portfolio companies when they are ready to raise their next round; later-stage VCs need to know early-stage VCs so they will see those companies; all VCs need to know same-stage VCs so they can share and syndicate deals; and everyone wants to know who is good at what—picking good deals, working with founders, exiting companies, and so on—so they can decide how seriously they should take various introductions. Not to mention, VCs trade in industry gossip, which helps them price deals, find great executives, find out about new sectors that are heating up and about sectors that are not panning out. VCs spend a lot of time having coffee or talking on the phone with other VCs so they can form relationships. These relationships make it much easier to do the job.

But being on a board with another VC gives another whole level of insight into how good or bad a businessperson they are. Knowing this, VCs who aren't very good businesspeople try to impress each other in board meetings by acting out their impression of one. Sometimes this takes the form of criticizing rather than critiquing, picking up on minor issues and making them seem more important than they are, micromanaging, and otherwise finding flaw with the CEO. Others may impress in the diametrically opposite way: They will spend the meeting on their phone or laptop, showing everyone they are too busy to be there. The latter is annoying but mostly harmless. The former can be disruptive.

Obviously, these are things you, as a board member, should avoid doing yourself. You can also help make things run more smoothly by calling them out in others (if you know how to do so without creating enemies).

DEALING WITH A BAD BOARD MEMBER, BADLY

Sometimes this isn't an act but is, in fact, who they are. I was the early-stage investor on a board with a couple of later-stage VCs and the CEO. One late-stage fund was in the midst of replacing their representative, an experienced partner, with a new partner at their firm. This new partner was fresh from selling his startup, which he had founded and grown to be very successful over ten years or so. Both the old and the new partners would come to meetings.

The new partner was used to being the person in charge, and in board meetings would respond to strategic discussion by going into great detail about what the CEO should do, how they should do it, how they should respond to anticipated problems, and so on. This clearly annoyed the CEO, who had been running the business for years, and made the board meetings very, very long. After a while, I couldn't take it anymore. "Maybe," I said, "you should go start another company instead of micromanaging this one." The new partner looked stunned, and it's true: I was being an asshole. The older partner laughed out loud and then smoothed things over.

I apologized after the meeting. And then the new partner apologized. "I'm still learning how to do this," he said. He did learn, and soon became the CEO's trusted confidante.

Antagonisms that start in a board meeting tend to persist afterward. It's hard for two people to settle their differences in front of a group. If you're one of the antagonists, sit down with the CEO and work it out after the meeting. If it's another board member, you can act as go-between if you have to. Remember, all you care about is the company succeeding. Put all the stupid stuff aside and focus on the goal.

FOUNDER VIEW: BOARD MEMBERS ARE OUTRAGEOUSLY SELF-INTERESTED

The dynamics that exist between investors are more complicated and interwoven than I ever could have imagined. There are three things I can consistently count on to be true:

1. Earlier investors will *never* screw over later-stage investors. They will not vote against them. They rely on them to write a check for the next round; their livelihood depends on it.

2. Later investors *will* screw over earlier investors. Anyone later doesn't need anyone earlier; the company already has their money, right? This means that later-stage investors won't hesitate to do things that are a gray area (or totally illegal) according to the IRA. They will protect their own capital by destroying others (including founders). I've even had Later Stage Investor say outright that they thought Earlier Stage Investor was an "idiot" and "useless." I shared it with Earlier Stage Investor. Did it change the fact that they always voted with Later Stage Investor? Nope.

3. Investors will always team up to vote against founders, and especially when the founder CEO is the target.

The reason I didn't recognize these patterns at the beginning of my career is because it requires time to see how all the politics play out. Relationships "change" over time or are simply laid bare for all to see, most likely in lockstep with how your company is doing.

AWFUL MESSAGES, WRAPPED IN SILK

One fun example I lived through was with an early investor. We had a close relationship, but as things became later-stage, it changed. The changes started with gentle suggestions of operational changes, and then escalated in a forty-five-minute phone call in which I was told directly that it was time for me to step down as CEO because (1) I want babies, (2) I can't raise babies while being a CEO because I'll have to travel a lot, and (3) I should take it from him because that happened to him while he was CEO. The message was delivered so beautifully, in fact, that I got off the phone and thought, "Wow, he really has my best interests at heart" for a few seconds before I shook off the fog and said *what the absolute fuck*. I immediately shared it with a co-founder and another investor and was cautioned by both to let it go. This was just a few years ago. One would think things are different now but they really aren't.

And so no matter how strong a foundation you believe you've created with your board members, they will always act in their own self-interests. They are beholden to returns (or sometimes their ego); it nullifies everything else you may believe you've built. Money rules over all of it. This perspective may sound jaded, circumspect, and pessimistic. It isn't; it's rooted in experience. The founder/investor relationship is often destructive, sometimes neutrally transactional (the ideal, in my perspective), and rarely positive. I've enjoyed all three.

INVESTOR VIEW: FOUNDERS SHOULD HAVE NON-BOARD ADVISORS

Sometimes what seems like self-interest in a board member is really just them putting the company ahead of the founder. This can feel like a betrayal to founders, though, especially if they have built a personal relationship. It shouldn't be surprising, because this is the board member's job; it just happens to coincide with the investor's job.

When the founder needs business help from someone, they might be leery of talking to a board member for this reason. It can be unwise to reveal weakness to someone with the power to fire you. The best people to talk to might be the early-stage investors.

Early-stage investors are more used to fluid situations, where processes are not yet in place and the facts that feed them are not yet known. If a CEO tells a later-stage investor that there is a problem and they don't know what to do about it, that investor might think the CEO is incompetent. But early-stage investors are used to this; they spend their time with CEOs in the first stages of a company, helping think through problems that do not yet have an answer. They are also the people who will have spent the most time with the CEO, so the CEO will most likely trust them more. And last, the financial interests of early-stage investors are more like those of the founders: Seed-stage equity usually has a very low preference and very few associated rights, so it is much more like common stock than late-stage equity.

Outside advisors can also be very useful. But they tend to be less engaged than investors, for two reasons. The first is obvious: The investor has more at stake. The second is that CEOs are busy and they neglect to keep outside advisors up to speed. If the advisor isn't current, the first ten solutions the advisor recommends will be the obvious ones the CEO already thought of and tried, but they didn't work. Investors are also more likely to be up to speed because knowing how and what the company is doing is part of their job.

FOUNDER VIEW: A CASE FOR OVERSHARING

I want to be surrounded by people with whom I can share everything. Pre-product market fit, the more minds, the better. Why bullshit when there's no business? Sharing is in everyone's best interests, and platitudes always suck. I try to have no bullshit in investor updates, no bullshit in board meetings, and certainly no bullshit one-on-one.

Here is an inexhaustive list of scenarios that I've personally experienced and which I've thought important to share with board members. I shared them because (1) they were things that involved the company, (2) I needed a sounding board to help me work through the scenario, or (3) I simply needed someone to talk to that had seen it before. While these items may paint me, co-workers, or co-founders in a bad light, they were shared *because* of faith in the process. I believed a board could be for good.

SHARING IS CARING

- A term sheet being pulled three days before the closing
- An investor's entire team taking me out to try to entice me to renege on a term sheet I'd signed three days earlier
- An investor refusing to put in their pro rata because they didn't like the way the founders were running the company
- A new investor pulling out a picture of a bunch of naked male torsos (pants on), covering their heads, and asking me which one was theirs in our first one-on-one dinner
- In that same conversation, the new investor pulling out a license to carry a concealed firearm that was impossible to get in their state of residence but they know the governor and so . . .
- A new executive whom we were worried wouldn't be manageable was indeed unmanageable
- Multiple investors repeatedly urging me to fire a co-founder across a period of years because he "sucked" and was "inauthentic"
- An investor putting his arm around me and kissing my forehead a block from our office

You'll notice a combination of scenarios: my bad judgment, investor conflict, sexual harassment, co-founder politics, and general business issues. Could I be more circumspect about things I share? Definitely. But I'd rather overcommunicate than under and that's a personal decision I made that's right for *me*. That decision has also been a net negative over time even if it has often worked to my advantage. Most people undershare with authority figures rather than overshare, because the more information that figure has about you or your decisions, the more they're apt to judge you based on things that are ancillary to the business or to use such information against you. I'd make the same decision again each and every time because it's how I want to do business. It's how I want to live my life. Lose the battle, win the war, they say. I suppose I choose the opposite.

I have theories as to why it's backfired on me. Most people are uncomfortable with raw honesty, especially the kind I listed earlier, and especially if the relationship is based in a business context. Another is that most people don't actually want to get to really know other people, or even know how. Men (generally) are uncomfortable talking about feelings, and especially those of a female operator. Instead of dealing with me as a whole person whose performance is affected by everything in my life (because for a founder, life and company are inextricably intertwined), they'd rather ditch me and find someone less challenging. But this is the wrong move because anyone who challenges the world is, by definition, challenging. That's why you wrote me a check, right?

INVESTOR VIEW: THE BOARD IS INVESTED IN THE COMPANY'S SUCCESS—NOT THE FOUNDER'S

I invest in people I want to succeed. It's why I started venture investing and why I do it now. But when I sit on a board, my job is to make sure the company succeeds. The company, not the founder. There's a difference.

I believe that, almost always, startups do better if they are run by the founder. But there are cases where the founder is strangling the company. When this happens, the board members try to change the founder's course. And when they can't, the only thing the board can do is change the founder.

CHANGING A CEO

One founder I worked with disliked managing, or even talking to, anyone but the software developers. He wouldn't hire salespeople or customer service people. The few customers he had were complaining. He desperately needed a chief operating officer to handle that side of the business. The board asked him to find one and he agreed.

The company hired a headhunter and for months couldn't find anyone qualified. The CEO would share applicant resumes with the board and, it's true, they weren't impressive. After a period of time it started to become ridiculous: I knew better COO candidates existed. I called the headhunter to find out why he wasn't finding these better ones. He was relieved I had called and complained that the CEO refused to meet the best candidates. I think the CEO was afraid of sharing his power with anyone else.

When confronted with this information the CEO insisted none of the "good" candidates would want the job. The board ultimately had to take on the task of finding and hiring someone. And since we no longer believed the founder would be open to that person being COO, we had to hire them as CEO. We asked the founder to stay as the chief product officer, but he decided he'd rather leave the business entirely.

The founder leaving, at whoever's initiative, is a huge deal, especially when the company is newer. Being the CEO of a small, venture-backed company is not a great job. You have all the outside pressure of running a big company, and all the frustration and lack of resources of running a small company.

This is the pitch to hire someone from the outside for the job: Here's a small company and a couple million bucks. Turn it into a big company quickly or we'll find someone who will. Until then we'll have monthly meetings to remind you that you are not on track.

Not very appealing, is it? It's almost impossible to find somebody talented enough to do the job who would want it. In addition, even if you do find them, they won't believe in the idea like the founder did. They also won't have the potentially huge windfall a founder might have if the company is successful (a founder at this stage probably owns somewhere between 30% and 70% of the company; if the board hires someone from the outside, the founder's stake doesn't go away, so the board can't offer the new CEO anywhere near that. They usually offer less than 10%). They just won't be as motivated.

Firing the founder is really bad for a pre-product-market fit startup. You exchange a true believer for a mercenary. A mercenary acts in their own best interests: They take far fewer risks and go for the easy revenue. This is a recipe for stagnation. The company may survive but will, as VCs say, be "going sideways." It will not be growing fast enough for an exit, so the VCs can't get their money out or even take the tax loss. All they can do is sit there and own a bunch of stock certificates worth something only in theory.

There are two times to remove an early-stage founder. The first is when, if they continue to run the company, the company will certainly fail (as in the previous example, where the founder refused to hire more people; or the example in the Fundraising chapter, where the founder refused to release the product). The other is when there is serious misconduct. This has to be dealt with, even though it might mean hurting the investment. You can't turn your back when a CEO—or any member of the company's management—is doing something wrong. (A couple of the things in Liz's long list of things-I-have-unwisely-informed-the-board-of raised my eyebrows, for instance, but you can't judge without knowing the details.) The idea that it might be a one-time thing, or that they can be chastised and it won't happen again, is always wishful thinking, in my experience. Do what needs to be done.

All of this, by the way, is for early-stage companies. Later-stage companies have different dynamics. They might be stable enough for an established executive to want to run, and they might have enough money to pay that person a market-rate salary. If so, they can hire an accomplished CEO. But why, you might ask, would they want to? If the founder took the company to that stage, don't they deserve the chance to keep running it? Yes, yes, they do. But when the VCs start to smell real money, real IPO money, the chance to get to a fund-returning exit can get the better of them. It's not personal, it's strictly business.

The bottom line is this: The CEO reports to the board, but the board should not run the company. The CEO needs to lead. This is what the board should want, what the investors will respect, and what is best for the company. Leadership requires having the board that enables, and even trains, the CEO to be the leader. It is only when the CEO can't or won't lead that a new CEO has to be found.

FOUNDER VIEW: BUILD YOUR OWN SHADOW BOARD

Founders getting fired is a real danger. Brad Feld and Mahendra Ramsinghani, in their book *Startup Boards*, say, "By the time the ventures were three years old, 50% of the founders were no longer the CEO."[1] I discuss safeguarding control (and therefore the founder CEO's job security) in the Terms chapter, so I'll avoid repeating that here.

Instead, knowing that's the case, I'd prefer to think about ways for me to do my job as best I can. I don't know what I don't know, and the board in its current manifestation doesn't help, so I instead create my own. I wouldn't be here today without oodles of folks paying it forward.

Liz's Board—let's call it my Shadow Board—is an unofficial group that makes up what I wish my board would be. It's a crowdsourced hodgepodge of folks who, like investors, are typically good at exactly one thing. Here are some archetypes I reach for:

- **A serial startup COO**: This is someone who's seen all investor bad behavior, can immediately deconstruct politics, and can also tell you exactly what you need to do operationally. My personal representative here also does it all in a British accent, which is even better.

- **Long-standing Seed investors**: This would be someone like my co-author or the first institutional investors to back the company. These people have also seen it all, twice. They're superb thinkers. They believe companies lose their value when founders are fired, are loyal, and dispense nuggets of wisdom that would never occur to you like, "The moment you think about firing someone, you already should have done it. So don't spend months obsessing about it." As one Pre-Seed investor is fond of saying, "The founder is my customer."

- **Any founder who's recently been through a later stage than where you are now:** There's a founder code among those who've been dragged through absolute fucking dirt. We won't talk about it unless we're asked, but when we do, watch out. From taking money off the table to politics to which investors are worse than others to complicated tax havens they've discovered, founders rock.

- **Co-founders:** For as much as you might bicker, if you get a founding team right, it's magical. Good founding groups complement each other, ideally in ways such that the middle of your combined Venn diagram is almost nil.

- **Therapists:** This isn't a CEO coach. This is someone with whom you can talk, and ideally one familiar with founder dynamics. They can be key to helping you manage internal relationships.

You'll find there's one missing archetype here: non-founder operators. I find them generally helpful but they are not part of my Shadow Board. I call them when I need specific advice, and I call twenty of them. They're like an index fund of ways in which things have been tried. For example, when we were building a customer success organization at one company, my co-founder called a number of operators to interview them on the ways they built their teams within the context of their product. He then used this pattern-matching to inform how we thought we should construct our own team. Their experience became our industry survey and we then chose the path that was right for us.

There *are* a few operators I've met and keep in the Rolodex who are exceptional. Guess what they go on to become? Founders.

INVESTOR VIEW: THE BOARD MEETING IS A PAGEANT

When I was a new VC I thought sitting on a board of directors was a sort of reward, a visible show of importance and respectability. I sponsored an investment in a company and would normally have taken the board seat. My boss "suggested" I put someone else on the board. They had particularly relevant experience in that company's market, and being on the board would motivate them to help the company. I was visibly annoyed. My boss rolled his eyes. "Nothing important happens in board meetings," he said. "The board is a waste of time, it's a fucking pageant."

What he meant was that I could provide better oversight by talking to the CEO outside the meeting. We could get to the important things immediately without the spectacle and politics a board meeting engenders. If you've ever sat through a bad board meeting, you can see how this would be true. But it's a waste of the founder's time for every investor to do this. Better to just make the board meeting more productive. He was right, though, that sitting on a board of directors is no prize. It's a lot of work that nobody's going to thank you for (except the other investors in the syndicate, who will thank you for not making them do it).

It's easy, when the money is flowing, for investors to let founders convince them not to have a board. But every time this happens, there's also a wave of founders who go off the rails (for every

WeWork, Theranos, FTX, or Uber, there are dozens more that didn't make the news) because of lack of oversight. VCs have to insist there be a board, and then work to make it effective.

FOUNDER VIEW: LEARN TO MANAGE YOUR BOARD OR YOU'RE TOAST

The board as it stands today is the manifestation of the legalese you signed when taking money, augmented with politics, relationships, and ego. As a founder, you can create a Shadow Board that can be truly helpful to you as an operator, but outside of the earliest Seed investors with whom you may become friends, it's hard to see a path to a genuine "real" relationship with your investors. You can cultivate strong and frequent communication, honesty to a point, and spend time at dinners enjoying yourself with them. You can get to a healthy, transactional relationship. You cannot, however, rely on this relationship to be real in the traditional sense. It simply isn't. It's a function of convenience for the investor, time-bound and event-bound, and in existence until you are no longer necessary.

And so, as a founder, and especially as founder CEO, you *must* invest time in learning how to manage them. Your job is at stake. Your company is at stake. Maintain that board to the best of your ability or it's going to get way *more* out of control.

KEY TAKEAWAYS

FOUNDER	INVESTOR
Boards are designed to fail. They are made up of people who have their own self-interests in mind, both VCs and founders.	The role of the board is oversight of the company. The board may also do other things that are important to the company's success, like give advice and help, but only if its members are managed correctly.
Board meetings are futile due to these self-interests and the fact that VCs are not operators.	Founders must be trained to use board meetings effectively, and investors must allow founders to run their companies without micromanagement.
Founders should find a way to mitigate this waste of time by trying to proactively manage their investors and minimize meetings.	Managing founders can be a delicate process. They will quickly dismiss board members who advance ideas that are poorly thought out or based on gut feel rather than data.
Board members are not your friends. They will always choose each other over founders.	Optimize toward the board members who are better at providing help and advice and who avoid micromanaging.
Create your own sounding board for what *you* need. The board is a pageant.	Remember that the interest of the board is making the company successful, not necessarily the founder.

5

GROWTH

INVESTOR VIEW: THE OPTIMIST'S DILEMMA

Two years after I first invested in Liz's second company, she went out to raise a new round. Several large VCs wanted to invest and they had bid up the price. The term sheet she was favoring valued the company at $300 million (these numbers are the right order of magnitude but are not the actual numbers; she's still under **NDA**, so she'd just have to edit them out anyway). I had an unusual worry: The deal was too good.

She gathered her co-founders and we borrowed a friend's office. I asked, "What does your company have to do over the next few years for this to be a good investment?"

1. The VC wants to at least triple their money in five years, the earliest you could reasonably expect to exit.

2. For the company to be worth more than $1 billion in five years, it will have to have at least $200 million in revenue.

Then I wrote six columns on the whiteboard, one for each year. I worked backward to a **triple-double** for the revenue. (The numbers here are millions of dollars.)

THIS YEAR	YEAR 1	YEAR 2	YEAR 3	YEAR 4	YEAR 5
$2	$6	$17	$50	$100	$200

I added rows for different types of employees: sales and marketing, software development, customer support, and so on. How many of each would they need to support that revenue each year? When we did this exercise, Liz and one of her co-founders were the only sales and customer support people. But if the revenue tripled, that would no longer work. We worked out how many people they needed to hire, plus the lead time it would take to find them, get them on board, and train them. Liz quickly realized that (a) hiring would be her primary job for the next five years, and (b) they were already six months behind.

This is the dilemma of every successful startup. Customers love the product, so founders get excited. Founders go to VCs to get money to grow into customer demand, and want a very high valuation. VCs calculate they can offer the high valuation if the company can grow very, very quickly. The startup gets the money. But they also get the expectation—the mandate, really—of high growth.

FOUNDER VIEW: PRODUCT MARKET FIT MEANS MORE PROBLEMS

You've found **product market fit** and it's time to scale. Congratulations! Most don't. Now forget all that and stop patting yourself on the back, because guess what? It's time to learn a whole new set of skills. And if you thought getting to product market fit was hard and that you've figured out the difference between life and death, you ain't seen nothing yet. Why? Because now you have something that people will pay at least one dollar for, and on a consistent basis. This means you are no longer a **call option** for your investors.

(If you don't understand what I mean, let me burst your bubble about Pre-Seed, Seed, and even Series A these days. To raise that money, you convinced people that you were smart or dogged or myopic enough to figure out how to take your idea and get people to buy it. Your investors' job is to sprinkle enough money around across enough companies such that if any of them make it to the stage you're at, they'll exercise those ever-so-valuable pro rata rights and call that option. They've gone from investing $2 or $3 million to $10 or $20 million and you're now no longer 1% of the fund; you're 10%. Call option over. Real life has begun.)

How does it manifest? Biweekly calls. Board meetings actually being called. Questions about burn and hiring and offices and retained searches and **COGS** and revenue and churn and customer acquisition and competition. There are a million questions that you don't have the answers to and nowhere near the expertise to even start thinking about how to attack. Your investors demand to know how you're going to turn their money into a massive company. You really just don't know. Even worse, you're not even sure how to get there. What got you from 0 to 1 isn't going to get you from 1 to 2. Your investors will be a broken record, asking the same questions over and over again. They'll offer up the same half-dozen introductions they always have—that temp CFO that comes highly recommended but pawns you off onto associates, that sales prospecting "expert" they have as an advisor to the firm who spouts jargon so well he was probably born that way, the former CEO of Insert Large Public Company Here that knew what it was like to operate twenty years ago but with limited relevance for today's enterprise SaaS startup, the executive coach that everyone uses who charges $1,000 an hour and sounds like she's reading a self-help book—all while ignoring the real question: How on earth do I help this founder child (because face it, we are) grow into a CEO when I myself am not one? That last part your investor will of course ignore.

And that, my friend, is the crux of going up and to the right. VCs will expect you to figure it out with their expert help and introductions, all the while willfully ignorant of the fact that these rent-a-humans are generally useless. They'll get frustrated when you mess up again and again and again, when things take twenty-four months when they "should" take twelve, that the market is "getting away from you," disregarding the fact that you don't actually have the majority of the tools you need in order to crush it. You'll argue about the symptoms of the problem. *You* will maybe be able to articulate the real problem; your investors definitely will not.

The problem is that you as founder are now much less useful. The company now needs you to be an operator. And not just any operator, but *the* operator, the one who can triple revenue for each of the next two years. And you don't know how to be that kind of operator. It's possible you ran a small team at your last company. It's possible you were a product manager. It's even possible you were CEO of another startup previously (I certainly was). But guess what? You don't know how to hire (well), to fire quickly (enough), to recruit, to run a management team (and especially one that gels), to manage the politics that can't *not* be present in the company (no matter how well the line "we don't have time for BS" in an interview lands, you do; it's there), and we still haven't touched on working with your investors, which means you also have to be a master politician.

In addition, your interests now start to diverge from that of your investors. If you are like most founders, you believe that you have a shot to sell early. The company is making real money and on an upward trajectory, which means that you're morphing from a pesky gnat to an actual thorn in the side of the behemoth you're trying to unseat. For your investor, you're now one step closer to being a real opportunity to pay back the fund and one that's now too big to ignore.

INVESTOR VIEW: STAGES OF GROWTH

As an investor, it's exciting when you see a company break through into product-market fit. It's like you've been driving around suburban streets and finally find the on-ramp to an open freeway.

But growth is hard. It's hard to get going, and once it's going, it's hard to manage. Founders might want to throttle it back, while investors are insisting that they can go even faster. Growth is what the founder signed up for, whether they realize it or not.

Paul Graham, the founder of Y Combinator, wrote an influential essay called "Startups = Growth." He says a "startup"—the kind of company venture capitalists like to fund—is different from all other companies that are started (hair salons, restaurants, dry cleaners, and so on)—because startups have to grow. If a startup wants to become a big, world-changing company in a short amount of time, then the most important thing they have to do is find a way to grow. Everything else follows from this: solving some customer's problem really well, having a quality product, a great team, a potentially big market, and so on. All these things enable a startup's rapid growth. The startup is irrelevant without the growth.

When they're raising money, some founders make overly rosy projections to get VCs interested, as Liz mentioned in the Fundraising chapter. They pitch to dozens of investors, and the ones that believe the predictions make the highest offers, because they have the highest expectations. The founder accepts the highest offer, implicitly endorsing these high expectations.

At some point, the founder might say, "We need to take a break from growth for a little while to fix some things." The VC's immediate suspicion is that the company has hit the limits of their growth, they vastly overpaid for the company, and they have to either get tough on the founder or cut their losses.

The VC's suspicions aren't really irrational. If you're at a slot machine that's somehow paying out pull after pull and you decide to step away for a moment to "fix some things," someone else is going to sit right down at that machine. Similarly, if you have a product that you have finally convinced customers they need and then you slow down selling it to them, someone else will step into your place. Before you existed, they didn't know about your better solution. Now they do. And so do your competitors.

Every sale you don't make is a sale someone else makes. Every day you stave off growth, that's growth someone else takes. And each time, the VC sees your market share and corresponding value, and their ultimate payday, get smaller and smaller.

Graham says there are three stages to a startup's growth:

1. The initial period of slow or no growth while the startup tries to figure out what it's doing.

2. A period of rapid growth as the startup begins to figure out how to make something lots of people want and how to reach those people.

3. Eventually, a period of slowing growth, as the successful startup grows into a big company.[1]

This is the iconic S curve that pops up sooner or later in every book about innovation.

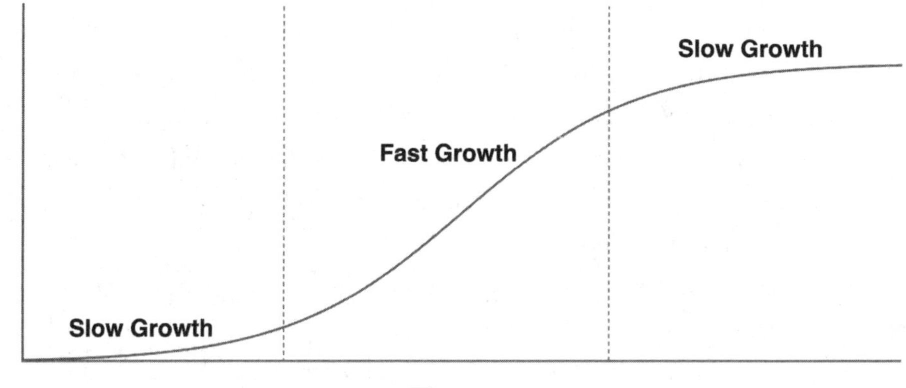

If a startup is in the first stage, the product isn't quite right for the market yet, and the entrepreneur won't be able to gin up real growth no matter what they do. But if the startup is in the second stage, where customers actually want the product, the only things blocking growth are standard operational problems: getting the product in front of potential customers, showing them it is what they need, signing them on as customers, and servicing them once they are. If the startup is in stage two, making sure these things get done is the founder's only job. And if they're not getting done, it is no one but the founder's fault.

FOUNDER VIEW: THERE'S ONLY ONE NUMBER ONE

Sometimes you can't grow until you "fix some things."

At the same time, Jerry's not wrong. Growth *is* critical. Investors want you to spend money as quickly as possible to win, without also running out of money. You're in a hot market, and so the faster you go, the odds of you becoming number one greatly increase.

You, the founder, might say, "Nah, there are definitely multiple winners in a category." Wrong. There's number one and then there's everyone else. There's a reason why venture capital funds are now registering at **RIAs** in order to have maximum flexibility in cashing out. The majority of upside now comes when a company goes public and so it's a race to IPO.

Let's take a fairly recent example in the identity (single sign-on) space: Okta and OneLogin. Both raised roughly $200 million. Both were started at the same time. Both do equivalent things. And yet one is worth $31 billion (at the time of writing), and one was acquired for, let's say, its last valuation of $330 million. That's right: Okta is worth ninety-four times that of OneLogin. It exited four and a half years earlier than OneLogin. It won, and OneLogin is a footnote in the market.

How did Okta do it? They both had roughly equivalent products and they both started raising at the same time in the same market. And yet . . . even by the Series A, in hindsight, you can see that Okta had already won. It raised $5 million more than OneLogin did, and then its B followed a year and a half later, while OneLogin's took just over three. Game over.

Okta: Total Funding $1.2 billion ($200 million pre-IPO)[2]

DATE	SERIES	MONEY RAISED
June 2020	IPO	$1 billion
September 2015	F	$75 million
June 2014	E	$75 million
September 2013	D	$27 million
December 2012	C	$25 million
August 2011	B	$17 million
February 2010	A	$10 million
September 2009	Debt	$750,000

OneLogin: Total Funding $175 million[3]

DATE	SERIES	MONEY RAISED
January 2019	D	$100 million
June 2018	C Extension	$23 million
May 2017	C Extension	$10 million
December 2014	C	$25 million
October 2013	B	$13 million
June 2010	A	$5 million

Okta won by deploying more capital more quickly. That's it. Through sheer force of capital deployment, it won. It became the proverbial downhill snowball that couldn't be stopped. As it moved into later stages, its fundraising served a second purpose: to suck all the wind out of the market. I'm not sure how many founders consider fundraising as a strategic play to suppress competition—I didn't for many years—but it's a highly effective technique. Nobody wants to invest in second place once a leader is anointed.

The same thing happened with Datadog and Loggly:

Datadog: Total Funding $150 million[4] (pre-IPO)

DATE	SERIES	MONEY RAISED
September 2019	IPO	$648 million
January 2016	D	$95 million
January 2015	C	$31 million
February 2014	B	$15 million
November 2012	A	$6 million
April 2011	Seed	$1 million

Loggly: Total Funding $47 million[5]

DATE	SERIES	MONEY RAISED
January 2018	Acquired by SolarWinds	Undisclosed Price
June 2016	D	$12 million
October 2014	C	$15 million
September 2013	B Extension	$11 million
July 2012	Venture Round	$6 million
May 2010	B	$4 million
February 2010	A	$500,000

Pick any enterprise SaaS category in the past ten years, look at the most valuable stock on the public market today, and you'll see the pattern repeated.

INVESTOR VIEW: SETTING UP FOR GROWTH

If founders and investors both believe in growth, what's the problem? Why is it such a flashpoint for conflict? Because founders sometimes *say* they believe in growth but are reluctant to do the things they need to do to grow.

Now that I've pissed off all the founders reading this, let me say that I understand. I do. Investors have a whole portfolio of investments, and only one has to work. Founders have just the one. If it fails, they fail. They want to make sure they don't run out of money, or that there's more coming if they do. Investors will never give them this assurance (if they're being honest). This means founders might want to spend the cash slowly and hope the market notices them, while investors may push to spend more aggressively. Investors want founders to swing for the fences. Founders might think that a series of base hits will do the job.

But we all know it won't. Liz makes the case that in sectors where fast growth is possible, you either grow fast or you lose. And if slow growth is a feasible strategy, *you shouldn't take venture capital at all.* Just do the work, grow the company, be the only owner, and enjoy getting rich without having a boss. Every founder should prefer this in any scenario where it's available.

Some founders need to grow fast. They raise capital knowing this, and then don't do the things to make it happen. This is usually because they don't know how. In this case, the VC can help. Not by telling them how to run their company, but by keeping the founder focused on some immutable truths about company scaling:

1. **You're building a company, not a product.** The first part of starting a company is the experimental phase: innovate,

test, repeat. When the startup finally finds a product customers want, this changes. It's not about thinking hard and being creative, it's about getting the product in as many customers' hands as possible, getting them to pay, and making sure it continues to satisfy. The company starts to have a bunch of customers with different needs, which is good. Each success or failure doesn't mean as much; their risk is spread out.

But it also means that at the end of the quarter, when the company has missed its growth target by 10%, the miss is composed of a bunch of little things that just didn't happen. This customer reduced their budget. That salesperson got a better job. This customer didn't close. That customer's contract is stuck in legal. This ad didn't work. That viral campaign didn't go viral. And so on. This is no longer bad luck, it's a systemic failure.

When it's systemic, the founder can't blame any one thing; they can only accept the fact that they haven't built the growth engine they need to build. That's on them.

Build that engine. Go from developing and selling a product to building a machine that develops and sells product. A machine takes a small input and turns it into a much larger output. Its parts are vision and people, and it uses money as fuel. The job of the CEO of a growth company is to design the machine, acquire the parts it needs, and feed it with money.

2. **You're selling to everyone, not just customers.** Founders know they have to sell to customers, and they've probably figured out they have to sell to investors. But they also have to sell to potential employees, existing employees, suppliers, partners . . . pretty much everyone. To do that, they have to have a compelling story.

The story is often codified in the "vision." Founders are the keeper of the vision. Having a vision lets them tell compelling stories. These stories convince customers, suppliers, partners, legislators, the media, investors, and—most importantly—prospective employees, that the company is doing something meaningful, useful, and inevitable. If they tell the story enough times, people will believe in the story and start telling it for them. Soon the company has built a brand, because a brand is really just a story that people already know, even if only subliminally.

The best founders love this part of the job, and VCs love that they love it. But founders sometimes forget how important the vision really is. They're tempted to think that they can buy talent with high salaries and stock options or that they can just go out and buy what they need to run the business from suppliers. And sometimes they can. But things you can buy with money are just commodities. If you want the good stuff, you need more than money. For instance, startups can either *hire* an employee or they can convince a superstar developer to *join* them. Joining is much more powerful.

USING VISION

Josh Reich, the founder of Simple, the neobank I backed in 2009, started the company because his bank had screwed him on overdraft fees. He complained, but got the runaround. All the banks he considered switching to had the same awful customer service, so he decided to start his own. It would be one that would treat its customers like customers.

This was a great story in the aftermath of the 2007-2008 financial crisis. People were angry at banks and wanted something better. Josh told this story many times, to a lot of people. Journalists contacted him to write newspaper articles about the company. This was essential free marketing early in the company's life. Out of the blue Josh got an email from Alex Payne, one of the top software developers in the country, saying he really admired what they were doing. A few weeks later Alex became their CTO. Josh's company never would have been able to *hire* Alex; he *joined* because he thought the company was doing something important.

Hiring is really hard. Hiring the best people is tough because they probably already have a great job at a great company. Founders have to convince them to leave their current job to join an unproven company. The pay probably isn't that much different, the stock options are a compelling dream but don't pay the rent, and they're joining a company they probably don't know a ton about because there's not a ton of information out there. But if they believe in the vision and feel like they can make a difference, they might take the risk.

3. **There's no return without investment.** One of the reasons founders hesitate to hire as aggressively as they should is the fear of running out of money. This can become especially evident when they reach the growth phase. Keeping expenses low when there's minimal revenue is good business. But once there's revenue to be had, companies have to spend money to get it. Sometimes it is

hard for founders to make this transition from careful to aggressive.

Mike Cannon-Brookes, co-founder of Atlassian, called this "ramen thinking": "We had a $50 million business, were generating $50 million ARR and $30 million a year in profit, and were growing at like 80% a year. Yet, we were of the mindset, 'We don't know if we're going to survive.' . . . We literally had $50 million revenue and $20 to $25 million in expenses; it was ludicrous, when I look back now. But mentally we were still in ramen days."[6]

When a VC raises money from their LPs, they can't just sit on it; they need to invest it. Otherwise there's no chance of making a return. The same is true for founders: If they raise money from a VC, the VC expects the founder will quickly invest it in growing the business.

4. **Get other people to do the work.** Every company needs to hire people to grow. There are no billion-dollar companies with only ten people. I like to do the exercise I did with Liz, which I mentioned at the beginning of this chapter, with founders entering the growth phase. We work backward from successful company to today, to see how quickly they have to hire people. Nothing else works quite as well to convince founders to focus more on recruiting.

HIRING AS COMPETITIVE ADVANTAGE

Founders who can hire are gold. I met the founder of one NYC-based tech company back when it was hard in NYC to compete with the financial sector for good software developers. I asked him why he thought he could hire enough good people there. He pulled out a notebook and turned to a page with a list of dozens of names. "I've already been recruiting. These people are excited to join. I'm just waiting for the money to pay them." I invested the next day.

> Hiring people to do the work isn't enough though. The only way to scale fast enough is to hire people who can hire people. I don't mean just an in-house recruiter, which isn't a bad idea, but that every time the CEO hires an executive, one of the requirements has to be how well and quickly they can hire good people. Founders sometimes take this for granted, but they shouldn't. Someone coming from a bigger company might be an excellent manager, but relied on HR to find all their hires. Look for people who have experience recruiting, interviewing, closing, and firing.

Your job as VC is to keep reminding founders that their job, once the company starts growing, is no longer to be chief cook and bottle washer, but to be CEO. They need to spend all their time and effort building the company.

My co-author would complain that founders know all this and VCs lecturing on what needs to be done rather than how to do it isn't helpful. I'd argue that many founders give lip service to these principles but don't really embrace their new job. They need to get it into their heads that they are building a company, not a product. All you can do as a VC is to pound it into them until it's bone deep. Of course they're not going to like it.

And, to founders wishing VCs would tell them how, not what: If someone gives you millions of dollars because you said you could get something done, you can't criticize them for not knowing how to get it done themselves. If they did, they wouldn't need you.

FOUNDER VIEW: IT'S ALWAYS GOING TO BE YOUR FAULT

I believe the job of the founder CEO is to spend money as quickly as possible to win without also running out of money. There's an asterisk, though: The company can't fall apart. Rather, it can only fall apart so much. Your asterisk becomes the crux of all tension with investors in scaling.

Scaling ultimately comes down to humans: Can I deploy capital quickly enough on people to win? Can I hire and train them faster (not even more effectively, just faster) than my competition to eke out an edge? Let's examine this, beginning with executive hiring. It's a favorite because it perfectly encapsulates the issue of covering all your bases in an area that's easy to mess up and still getting fucked anyway for it.

You need to create a management team in order to scale. Unless you're lucky and outrageously well-connected and can pull in the right folks when you need them (or before), you'll go with an executive search firm and most likely one your investors recommend.

There are many retained search firms and there's no such thing as a good firm; there are only good recruiters. In my book, the definition of a good recruiter is fourfold:

1. They get to know you and your co-founders well, which means that they'll be that much more effective at finding someone who will be a "culture" fit. Because culture is such a fuzzy word, let's define it here as "someone whose

personality will jibe well with founding team dynamics and especially someone you'll actually like."

2. They are effective (enough) at figuring out (enough of) what you do such that they can represent your company well (enough) to get the candidate to take a call with you. That means limited jargon and certainly not making it seem like they're reading from a piece of paper. I had a top recruiter recently reach out to me to see if I wanted to be CEO of a company he represented. When I asked him to explain in plain English what the company did (because their website sure as hell didn't), his eyes kept moving back and forth as he read the boilerplate statement he was given, which of course didn't explain anything at all. It was hard not to snicker.

3. They've been through enough of these such that they know how to disqualify quickly and push back when candidates are asking for things out of the ordinary and wildly off-market. For example, if a VP Sales candidate is asking for 3 points fully diluted on a Series A, one of the following scenarios is true: either someone has (1) given that to them before in wild desperation, (2) they think they're such hot shit that they can get anything, (3) they are mistaken about the market, or (4) all of the above.

4. They're honest and actually working for *you*. I had one recruiter lie directly to my face about the compensation a candidate was asking for because the search had gone on longer than she expected and she was desperate to close it and get paid. Note that this was silly in every way: In addition to her reputation being sullied when folks would back channel to me before signing with her (her fault—she put

> my company's logo into her pitch deck—which goes to show exactly how much brain power was there), she would have had to replace the candidate if and when they failed (retained search firms guarantee a redo typically within three months of the start date).

It's nearly impossible to find all these qualities in a single person, so try to get two and then augment what's missing with co-founder or investor help.

EQUITY DEMANDS FROM VULTURES

Let me also comment on the disgusting trend that has developed over the past few years with recruiters. Executive search firms used to charge $100,000 to $125,000 per search. Now they ask for either fully vested common stock on search completion, a warrant to invest in the next round, or both! Their logic is, "We're invested in your success and want to do so next to you, dollar for dollar," but in fact, it's a shitty, self-serving way to get on the cap table of promising startups that essentially creates a new type of Silicon Valley index fund!

You have the ability to push back. You can say no, say your board won't allow it (this excuse always makes me chuckle), or that you'd be happy to consider it on the next round, but for the time being they need to prove themselves because so many other recruiting companies want the same deal, so it's a bit of a dogfight. Use your negotiating skills and just say no, kids!

It's also critical to note that more than 50% of executive searches fail. Let that sink in. *More than 50% of these searches fail*, which means at least half your time in this area will be wasted. You'll hire the person, they'll come in, and something won't be right. Maybe it was something small you picked up on in the interview process but ignored. Maybe it was the risk everyone identified that came true. Maybe you took a chance on someone young and hungry who actually couldn't jumpstart an entire department. Or the inverse happened, and you hired someone with twenty years at Oracle who wanted to "go early" and then abysmally sank in the nebulous cloud of startup uncertainty. It will happen.

Investors will ask to be a part of these searches. And they should be. They can be helpful simply because they've interviewed a number of these types of candidates in their career. They can also definitely help you sell a candidate hard who's on the fence, and the more storied the investor, the more awestruck the candidate will be. Note that you shouldn't expect a ton of insight from those who've never operated, but they want to be "helpful," and simply by you letting them talk to the candidate, they will feel better about themselves.

So you say, "Yes! Please help me recruit these folks in." You've covered your bases. Investors feel like they've had a say and are important, you get their blessing, everyone's on the same page. Note that I said that you'll get their blessing. You will, 100% of the time. I've yet to experience or hear about a single investor, either directly or anecdotally, disqualifying a single candidate they've been sent.

Once you've hired and onboarded the executive, reality hits. Your candidate is not performing. Rather, the indicator that says whether or not they're performing isn't moving, or it's not moving fast enough for your investors' appetite, or their personality isn't meshing well with the team.

Two examples from my past:

1. We interview for a VP to "build a team from scratch." Our choice was young, hungry, personable, and saw the opportunity to make their career. We loved this person's background because they were well-versed in their subject area, started their career at the bottom and worked their way through every position in the division, *and* came from a company that had both a bottoms up and top down motion. Everyone signed off, including our management team and all investors on the board. Product market fit had already been identified; "all" that needed to happen for this person to succeed was training and hiring. Another executive and I got alarm bells in the last stage of the negotiation because the person came off as tone-deaf. We were talked off a ledge by the other folks involved. The VP joins and proceeds to spend the next few months (1) not hiring a single full-time employee, (2) hiring a consultant to outsource training, (3) frustrating another executive by outsourcing work without asking *that* executive's team, (4) alienating existing staff by talking down to them, and (5) bringing up product-led growth as the future in every management team meeting. In a conversation with HR regarding flagging team morale, the VP ruminated that it would be "damaging to their brand" if they were to get fired. I decided it was time to let this person go. In the termination conversation, this person said, "Well, I also don't feel like [SUCH AND SUCH] is my job and I don't enjoy it; that's for marketing." Yowza.

2. We interview for another VP. The search went on for four months; nobody seemed senior enough. We went to adtech, agencies, traditional SaaS, everywhere. We decided to level down and look at hungry directors. We found a young, hungry, and poised candidate who knew how to

> manage budgets, and better yet, came with a team! (Note: If you're hiring an executive and their team doesn't follow them, they're not much of a leader. This was another unknown mistake we made with the first VP. Surprised that our investors never brought it up as key? I'm not.) The candidate had been through a scaling startup and acquisition. The back channel references returned positive. Everyone was onboard. Three months in: nothing. No chutzpah, no confidence, no initiatives accomplished save a migration that was already in progress when they started. The person quit and got a job as a VP at a smaller startup with lower stakes.

What were the things that we missed?

In the case of the first VP, we had a hint of arrogance in the offer stage but ignored it. Nobody, and I mean nobody, considered that this person was used to having leads fed to them, having come from one of the few companies that perfected **PLG**.

In the case of the second VP, everyone missed the key problem: This person had been a director for three months before we extended the title of VP. They had never gone this early, which had serious implications for building an outstanding program. They just couldn't start from scratch. Zero to one is not one to two.

As CEO, did I mess up on both of these? Yes. Did each slow down the growth of the company? Hell yes. Did all board members and founders and key investors and company executives sign off on the hires, often with forceful enthusiasm? Yes.

And did I get blamed for them all? You already know the answer to that question.

I believe I play politics well, most of the time. Let me be clear: No matter what you do when hiring executives, no matter how passionately the board agrees with the decision, if these hires fail, for whatever reason, it is your fault.

Executive hiring exemplifies the tension with the board. You have to get these hires right at the right time. The board sees only the broad strokes. To quote Cher from *Clueless*: "It's like a painting, see? From far away, it's okay, but up close, it's a big ol' mess." They will see the hire, see it not work out, and believe that it's your fault. Lots of it will be (and everything I just mentioned excludes all the mistakes I made, which include being overbearing, not letting go of enough soon enough, asking too many questions, the list goes on and on) but it ignores the fact that often the candidate just isn't a fit. It's not the broad strokes that make teammates work; it's the details. And the board doesn't see the details and doesn't care to and certainly doesn't have empathy for them. The board just wants results and if you don't produce them, get ready for unpleasant times.

Let's take another example of scaling conflict: When is the "right" time to hire salespeople?

Your board will tell you to hire **AEs** as soon as you've made a few sales. They'll see a bit of revenue, the potential outline of a replicable sale, and they're like, "Let's go!" Great instinct, but the dumbest thing you could do for two reasons.

First, sales folks are good at selling something that has a playbook. You do not hire them to figure out your playbook. You hand them the memo and say, "Go do this." I learned this lesson at my first startup. I poached the top salesperson from the company I had left and gave this person a VP Sales title. The sale was markedly similar (same commodity, adjacent space) but the person couldn't get it done. They didn't know how to justify the value, but that's beside the point. It simply wasn't fair of me to ask that of them, and I certainly didn't know that at the time.

Second, hiring salespeople isn't just hiring salespeople. It's defining a process and workflow and figuring out who you need. Is it enterprise? Mid-market? Do they need a background in prospecting? Will cold callers work or do we need relationship builders? What's the sales cycle? You just won't know at this stage. You also won't know how to manage them (and these gentle egos are in sore need of massaging) and how handoffs happen between sales and customer success and different ways to price . . . I could go on and on.

I once made the mistake of hiring AEs about a year too late, and then once we did, we didn't have sufficient training or mentorship in place to make sure they were successful. We eked it out (in no small part thanks to their fortitude). If I were to do it again, I'd hire the infrastructure before anything else. We did this with HR, actually, and kudos to a co-founder for having the foresight to insist on it. That plumbing, the ability to lubricate the experience, was a move critical to adding personnel successfully after being only eight employees for a long time. Looking back, I'd have done the same thing for sales: education first, AEs second (or simultaneously).

Going back to the board, they'll think you're nuts. They'll say, "Hire AEs! What are you waiting for?" They want you to scale *now*. You see that these folks will spin their wheels without a playbook. In this situation, I actually believe the two sides can find some middle ground. Your investors have those sexy ex-salespeople they reach out to for advice. Get that connection! Use that person politically. They can listen to your calls, tell you what else you're missing, and know that they're reporting back to the board. Wonderful. If they're smart (and they most likely are), they'll immediately see where you are struggling, and it won't be on selling. You, as founder CEO, can sell like the dickens. You probably have issues with prospecting or pricing or starting with a larger initial deal size or whatever, all components of the playbook. Take your time, refine them, let this sales prince look over your shoulder and tattletale on you. You look like a champion for being "coachable" and you buy yourself time to feel confident there's enough playbook from which to hire.

Net: You'll have a hard time hiring executives. When they fail and you have to fire them, the board will blame you, even if the hire was vetted by them. There's no way around it. Still, do try.

INVESTOR VIEW: GETTING THE FOUNDER TO LET GO

Founders are nuts, that's what investors love about them. And, just like with any other person you love, the only useful thing you can do when they start to act irrationally is listen and try to figure out what's really going on. They say it's lonely at the top, and this is especially true when you're at the top of a startup. Founders have sold everyone on their half-baked vision, and every time something goes wrong, everyone looks to the founder to know what to do. The founder, of course, often doesn't know either. You need to be the person they can work it through with.

This doesn't mean *you* need to know what to do—in truth, the founder probably does know, they just need someone to help them understand that. And understand that their job is to come up with strategies and get their people to execute them. They need to become a manager.

Managing the company to grow means giving up most day-to-day operational activities. This is a problem for most founders, who have a hard time completely entrusting the things they have been spending all their time doing to someone else. After all, if they made it this far, they were probably really good at them. Some founders are product geniuses, and they have to entrust product management and design to someone they hired. Some founders are technical whizzes, and they have to entrust technology development to someone else. Some founders have a way with customers, and they have to entrust marketing and sales to someone else. And, seeing as the founder had the passion and vision to focus on what they were good at for the years needed to get the company to the growth stage, and were good enough to get the company there through the toughest kind of times any manager ever sees, the person they hire is almost certainly not as good at it as they were.

But how big would Microsoft have gotten if Bill Gates insisted only he could be in charge of writing code? How big could Google have become if only Sergey and Larry could be in charge of what the product was? At some point, if some important thing can be done only by the founder, the founder becomes the bottleneck to continued growth. (Steve Jobs in his later incarnation may be the exception. So, if you're Steve Jobs, you can ignore this part.)

The founder has a legitimate interest in things being done as well as possible. They may decide to slow growth because they want to make sure the product, the technology, the marketing is all top-notch, and the only way to do that is to be personally involved. This is understandable, but unsustainable.

Starting a company and scaling a company are completely different jobs. As a founder you have to switch from *doing* to *managing*, and this is harder than it seems. And you also have to switch from the exploring mindset to the commercializing mindset. You have to manage a growing company and manage the company to grow.

I once asked Jeff Dachis—co-founder of Razorfish, who in four years grew it from two people to more than twelve hundred, spread across five countries, and took it public—what changed about his job as the company got bigger. He told me the job changed radically three times: when their headcount exceeded forty or so people, when they opened their second office, and when they went public. The last two I could see, but the first he had to explain. When the company was small he knew all the people. He and his co-founder had personally hired all of them. They spent all day together and went out after work. They survived the ups and downs of startup life together, forging the ties that can only be forged striving side-by-side. But one day, when the company was about forty people, he saw someone in the office he did not know. One of his managers had hired them without his involvement. This was by plan, of course—he had delegated some hiring and managing—but it didn't make it any less strange. He had to reconcile himself to managing people who managed people. He had to trust the people he hired to do part of the job he had once done. This was very, very hard. But he did it, and the company grew to become the leader in their field.

Managing a growing company means you usually can't do the work anymore because you're too busy managing people who are doing the work. When you start a company, you wear all the hats. At my startup I once spent the first half of the day pitching world-renowned venture capitalists and the second half trying to get the security system at our new office working so the cleaning staff could get in at night. I also talked to customers, reviewed technical specs for the product, interviewed potential hires, and spent long hours with my co-founders debating what the product should be. But once the company got bigger, there were other people who did those things, and I became one of the bureaucrats managing and keeping track of them.

WANTING TO MOVE ON

An old friend, who has also been a founder, told me he was relieved to be replaced as CEO of his startup. He loved starting the company and building the product, but once it started to get traction with customers and grow rapidly, he felt out of his depth. Hiring, managing, selling, and the politics of dealing with a larger workforce were just a grind to him. But he felt trapped. He knew that if he told the board he wanted to replace himself, he risked losing control of the process, potentially being pushed out, and having his ownership diluted.

When his company and another both looked to be growing into becoming direct competitors, he saw his opportunity. He negotiated a **merger of equals** that graciously allowed the founder of the other company to become the CEO of the combined company. By doing it this way he had the leverage to keep some control, avoid dilution, and come off looking like a hero to his investors. It was a clever solution to a difficult problem.

Replacing a founder as CEO, if not done carefully, can alienate the founder. This creates tension with the employees (who the founder had a hand in hiring) and potentially with customers and other investors. It also means the company loses the crucial know-how that was in the founder's head. Every time I have seen a founder fired it has led to severe negative consequences for their company. Some have survived and some have failed, but almost all take a hit to their business.

Finding a merger of equals may be the most elegant way to do this, but I've seen other ways: kicking the founder upstairs to be chairman of the board, or moving them sideways to be head of product, for instance. I have even seen VCs help the founder leave to start an entirely new company, where they can do what they love best: building. All these things keep the founder friendly, engaged, and helpful during the transition, and this is the key to minimizing disruption to the business.

VCs can only credibly help find these outcomes if the founder trusts them. The founder must believe the VC cares about more than just their own interests, that they take company-building seriously, and that they will keep their word. To be trusted when a founder transition is happening, when emotions and suspicions are fraught, the VC has to have earned this trust by being consistent about their responsibility and accountability to the company since the very beginning.

It's an old VC cliché that the job of the startup CEO is to set the vision, raise capital, and hire employees. This will end up taking all their time, and a good CEO of a growth-stage company realizes this and optimizes around it. It's hard to overemphasize how big this psychological transition can be for some founders. You, the investor, can't fall into the trap of thinking there's something wrong with them for struggling with it. There's nothing wrong with them; you just have to help them get past it.

FOUNDER VIEW: IT'S SO HARD TO SAY GOODBYE TO YESTERDAY

I agree with Jerry on everything except the investor piece. They aren't capable of helping and won't help the founder get through it. The investor cares only if the company is going up and to the right. Case in point: There are plenty of startups I know of where internal goings-on were a shit show and yet the VCs were fine with it because the company was hitting its numbers.

In making the leap from doer to manager, the founder has to admit they're flawed. I do lots of things wrong. The hardest thing I had to learn was to let go. You *have to* hand off to folks who will help you scale and some of that is handing off things you *really* care about. For example, I am a stickler for grammar. I am also a decent writer. And I firmly believe when selling that you do not talk about yourself (or your company) in the first person. Nobody cares about you; they care about themselves. Now throw in the brand identity of the startup I spent so many years crafting, and Disaster, here I come!

This was no more marked than when my company published its technical documentation online. They were originally authored by the head of support. He could write, was also a bit insane about grammar, and followed instructions (no first person). We eventually hired a technical writing team (scaling means handing off). This team (1) wrote verbosely and (2) didn't have the best grammar. Why did we hire them? Well, they were doing their job as content producers. Their responsibility was to write hundreds of web pages outlining how to use the product. Their job was to keep documentation up-to-date. Their job was to expand our SEO footprint because our perspective was that technical documentation *was* marketing. Their job was *not* to write beautifully.

I freaked out. I insisted every page get edited and reviewed by another team member. My co-founder and I had argument after argument about the problem. I didn't understand why it was so hard to have an MVP align to some sort of brand standard, and I didn't understand why the writing team couldn't accept *my* brand standard. I was the CEO, after all. My co-founder didn't understand why I insisted on a refined product when we were in the early stages of scaling (Google indexing our words meant growth; up-to-date documentation meant faster deployments and less stress on the Support team). I nearly vomited when I read the style guide that was eventually authored. The first sentence of the grammar section started with the present progressive! Our compromise was to hire an editor, but then the writing team wanted to debate the edits. The company was stuck in a vicious cycle and it was my fault.

My co-founder was right in those early moments. The team needed to feel ownership over their work product and the company needed them to churn out accurate docs. We could hire an editor later. Could you argue then you'd probably need to undo a lot of the behaviors that were to become entrenched (e.g., an ability to argue with an editor)? Definitely. But that wasn't the battle that was necessary to fight then.

I asked the original docs author what his thoughts were on this process:

I had a similar experience but on another topic.

When I handed off docs to the new team, it was a relief: not just because you were always looking over my shoulder every time I made changes, but because it was becoming too much of a distraction from what I was actually hired to do, which was handle customer support issues. I couldn't really understand why you were spending so much time focusing on the docs like that since I assumed—correctly?—you had better things to do with your time. But I had my own blind spots, of course.

Where I had problems was in handing off customer support issues to someone else. My first hire, as I'm sure you'll remember, was technically great but nowhere near as . . . let's say pedantic . . . about things like grammar and style. That led to a lot of conflict at first because I just couldn't understand why they couldn't seem to write support emails like I did. We spent hours of frustrating time together—both for them and for me—trying to get those emails up to my existing standard, and never really managed it. And if I remember correctly, one of the reasons we spent so much time on it was because you were super annoyed by those emails too. I don't think it was until I hired my second support engineer, with their own writing style and preferences, before I was able to realize that I'd been focusing on the wrong thing.

Look, when customers write in with a problem, they need the problem solved. They don't give a shit if the support person is emailing them messages full of split infinitives and missing commas. They want to be able to read the message, understand it, and get a solution. All the rest is gravy. Not just gravy, but a special kind of gravy that only some people can actually taste and appreciate. A lot of folks just don't care, and that's fine. Even the folks that care a lot aren't going to ding a technically accurate support response for grammatical issues. I certainly don't when I'm asking for technical support.

But getting to that point took a lot longer than it should have, because I had a hard time letting go and seeing the big picture. It's not just founders with this problem! ”

"It's not just founders with this problem." It's not.

A similar pattern repeated with one of my sales teams. The founders had discovered that precision (in notes, in listening, on calls, in memory) was key to closing business that stuck around. Our buyer was discriminating and didn't take kindly to words being put in their mouth. The sales team chafed hard at this requirement early on. A year later, they called me up complaining about how the new sales hires wouldn't listen to the fact that they had to take fastidious notes, and deals were at risk because of assumptions that arose from the lack of rigor. I laughed at the irony.

Ceding responsibility, especially operationally, is hard and it's directly correlated to the amount of time you've invested. How many times have you interviewed someone and three or four calls in, there's something wrong but you can't quite put your finger on it so you keep going and then probably hire them? Let's call it the Fat Folder syndrome and it's emblematic of the worst issue a founder faces: letting go.

Letting go requires a founder CEO to look at every decision dispassionately. We often fail at moments like this. There are thousands of these decisions that have to be made a month. If you go with your gut and deep-seated values (in the case of writing), you'll lose. If you try to get total consensus (as in the case of executive hires), you'll also lose. It ends up being a no-win situation that requires finesse every time. Assume you'll lose even as you engage in the pointless exercise.

INVESTOR VIEW: IF VCS KNEW HOW TO RUN A COMPANY, THEY'D BE RUNNING A COMPANY

I don't want founders to be dispassionate, I want them to go from being passionate about their idea to being passionate about growth. Granted, being passionate about growth is not anywhere near as inspiring as being passionate about solving one of the world's problems (big or small as it may be), but it's more exciting. The founder who can turn their focus from "solving this problem for a few people" to "solving this problem for a lot of people" is the one who is going to make a difference.

The biggest opportunity founders will ever have is growing their company. It's hard to start a company, and harder to get it to product-market fit. Few people get there. If you're one of them, if you're the first to market with a product that customers really want, you've won the lottery. Don't dither around wondering if you should cash in the ticket.

VCs can help, but only in specific ways. If you want advice on what your company has to look like to be considered valuable, ask the VCs. If you want advice on how to actually do that, I agree with Liz that you will get plenty of advice that probably has very little applicability.

When they're trying to invest, VCs tell a good story about how they can help the founder figure out what to do. They claim to be master strategists, with skills honed through exposure to scores of companies. But think about this for a second: Go look at the list of the richest people on Earth. How far down the list do you have to go before you find a VC? Pretty far. How far do you have to go to find an entrepreneur? Not far at all. Every one of the twenty richest people on earth in 2021 have their money by founding a company, being married to a founder, or being descended from a founder. All of them.

VCs are not operators. If a VC could operate better than you, they would be operating. That's where the money is. Many VCs were operators once, of course, but the half-life of that knowledge is pretty short. As a rule of thumb, VCs probably have decent operating advice for about half the time they were operators. That is, if they were the CEO of a company for ten years then they probably have decent advice for about five years after they become VCs.

VCs can help when you're raising money, by making introductions to other VCs, by committing to invest in the round, and by vouching for you. They can help a little bit with the brand-building; if they're a well-known VC, their bet on you may help convince some potential partners, customers, and employees that you are worth taking a bet on. But this is icing on the cake. You still need to be the cake. It's not what founders want to hear after the VCs promised all sorts of help during the investment process, but scaling is the founder's job, not the VC's.

FOUNDER VIEW: HARDEN OR YOU'RE TOAST

There is one more thing to consider. As a founder, you must go through a change in which you stop thinking about people as people. There is a reason why it's called human capital. We've discussed that you hire people to deploy them, and people doing things means making money. This requires a shift in your psyche. It requires you to develop sociopathic tendencies (which I believe most founders already have). I am not a sociopath but I do have inclinations. I ask about peoples' days and tell them to take time off if they're sick or lagging, but don't think about it beyond that. Do I care? Yes, I want them to feel well, but I care more about them doing great work. Do I feel bad when I fire someone? Yes-ish? I empathize that their life has been upended, having been let go myself earlier in my career, but it is also true that the moment poison or underperformance is gone, things just work better.

I was dating someone during a period of growth and my boyfriend was disturbed again and again by the way I spoke about decisions regarding employees. He'd fret about how quickly we'd hire and fire, or the way in which us co-founders would discuss executives and in the plainest of terms. He'd say, "But they're people." He was right and is right. At the same time, I had to harden. Decisions have to be made independently of feelings. The company becomes an entity unto itself and to do right by it means disassociating humans from the capital. And the reason it's called human capital is that people have been commoditized. Running the company requires a form of sociopathy. And that's where the founder transition to operator typically fails.

Everything I've written here—*none* of this an investor would ever talk to me about. None of it and none of them. I had an investor who was an extremely successful CEO. He never brought any of this up. And this was someone who turned over his entire management team at least once on the way to IPO. For investors, it's always, "Why haven't you hired everyone?" You, the investor, expect me to figure it out because I have managed to birth this company into the world, and yet there are people who devote their entire life to the craft of getting it right. And you, the investor, don't care about that minor implementation detail; I just need to figure it out or get fired.

I find this odd to say the least. Investors should care about providing you with help to figure all this out. They should work their asses off to make sure you (aka their investment) are successful. Similar to me messing up an operational mistake and putting the company behind by six months, wouldn't the investor not want to lose time? But they, like you, have only a certain amount of attention and energy and will and many more investments than just you. Some funds now have pods of folks that swarm around you to help spot your weaknesses (especially on the revenue function), but even that gives me pause. I can't trust my investors and so why trust their proxies with the company's most intimate issues? I've found it's a mistake to do so. And so scaling the company to be bigger faster requires the founder to become a whole new person.

Growth is scary from this light: It means that if I don't figure it out, I'm gone. That has the potential to introduce fear into a CEO's decision-making process. It becomes key for the founders to keep their eye on this tendency.

Let me end on a note about fatigue. Founders get tired. Scaling is exhausting, made more so because it takes even more energy than everything up until this point. Going from 0 to 1 is exciting; I've found nothing like it. Then you've got to figure out how to hand it to a bunch of other people to scale it. That requires emotional growth, which may be even harder than the scaling itself. With the scaling also comes those investors, now more interested in the outcome because the money has now become real. VCs are better at telling founders what to do rather than telling them how to do it because they just don't know. And yet you're damned if you do and damned if you don't because these investors don't care about any of it except the results.

Remember: Your board has long memories of failures and short ones of successes. You're fucked.

KEY TAKEAWAYS

FOUNDER	INVESTOR
Growth means the big leagues. Your job is to deploy capital quickly without running out of it.	VCs invest in startups that (both implicitly and explicitly) promise to be high-growth companies. They then hold founders to this promise.
Founders need to become good at operating, which is really hard. VCs are the last to prepare you for it and will blame you for failure.	VCs aren't operators and are not that useful for operating advice. That is not the help they can give, despite what they promise up front.
Everything is outrageously hard, especially hiring. No matter what you do, you will mess it up and your investors will blame you.	If the startup is in a position to grow and it doesn't, investors will blame the founder. If a founder CEO gives up on or backs off from growing the company, investors may decide they need a new CEO.
In order to scale, founders have to let go of doing everything. This means hiring people to take over parts of the founders' jobs.	VCs can help by keeping the founder focused on growth. This usually means convincing the founder to hire and delegate.

6

EXITS

INVESTOR VIEW: THE MOMENT OF DECISION

Yahoo! tried to buy Google in 2002 for $3 billion. This would have been a huge windfall for the founders and the venture investors. Google said no—its founders believed they were worth much more—and went public two years later with a valuation of $23 billion, a much bigger windfall. Without the benefit of hindsight, turning down a multi-billion-dollar offer seems crazy, but it's the kind of crazy venture capitalists love.

Venture capitalists like to say that venture capital outcomes follow a power law. If you ranked a particular fund's exits biggest to smallest, the biggest would be about twice the value of the next biggest, which would be about twice the third biggest, and so on. About halfway down the list, the exits have gotten small enough to round to zero. This means the largest exit is worth more than all the other exits combined. It's like playing the lottery: You lose almost all the time, but when you win, you win big.

The following graphic charts all of my exits—both the good ones (made money) and the bad ones (lost money, sometimes all of it). I pride myself on having relatively steady returns; I've had roughly the same **return on investment** for the last twenty-five years and I make money on about half of my investments. Even so, you can see that a single investment dictated my overall returns.

Most VCs have a slightly less exaggerated curve. But even for them, that one exit probably returns everything the fund invested; the other exits are the gravy. For nine out of ten great VC funds, if you removed the best-performing company, they would no longer be considered more than mediocre. That goes for me too. A fund might invest in twenty companies or a hundred, but it's that one investment that makes or breaks the VC.

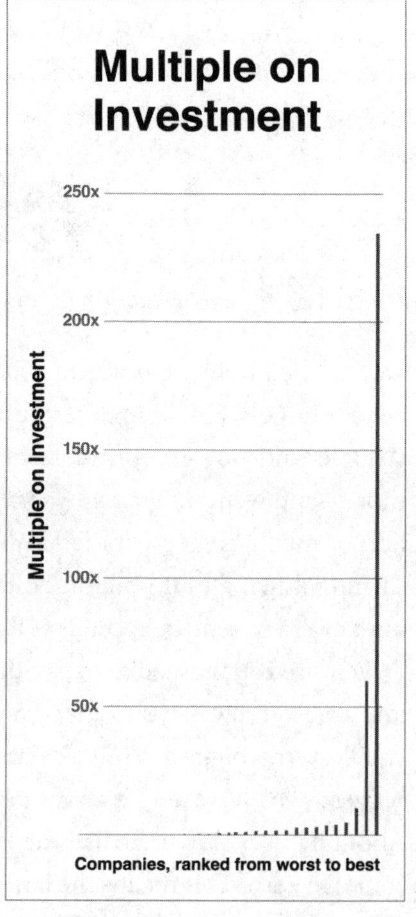

Venture capital is like going up to bat in professional baseball: You are constantly and ruthlessly reminded that you are usually wrong. But unlike baseball, where a hitter might face tens of thousands of pitches in their career, a VC might make their reputation on the few dozen companies they are deeply involved in and retire having backed, if they're lucky, a handful of big wins. This isn't enough to notice any statistical regularity, so it warps the VC's thinking in truly strange ways. Most of why a company succeeds or fails is completely out of the VC's control. The few parts that are in their control they focus on intently.

When you can't predict your luck, you are left with trying to improve your odds. And almost all VCs, when faced with an outcome not to their liking, will decide, to the founder's horror, to roll up their sleeves and "help." But even the VCs that have had operating experience aren't very good at fixing things. In the end, VCs are money managers, so there are only two times in the life of a company they can really affect their outcomes: when the company raises money, and when it exits. During the former, of course, it's all wine and roses because the opportunities are limitless. But when it comes time to exit, it becomes a zero-sum game, and the knives come out.

FOUNDER VIEW: NEVER FORGET YOUR FUCK YOU NUMBER

At the beginning of my last company, my co-founders and I shared what number each of us would need to make in order to agree to sell the company. Every founder has a number and it's silly to pretend otherwise. We did it so we knew exactly where we all stood if an offer were to come. We called it our "fuck you" number. Each person's number was based on their personal opinion of what it would take for them to be totally free of external demands. Our numbers were wildly divergent.

Unlike investors, a million dollars can change your life. As a founder, you may start your company because you truly believe in the vision. You may start it because you lust for money. If you're lucky, both coincide. Our definition of fuck you money differed based on what we wanted to do with it, but no matter what, *a million dollars is a lot of money.* Don't let *anyone* tell you differently, especially not your investors.

When you're starting out, your company is valued at $5 million or $10 million and you're a call option for the VC. Nothing seems real. Earning even $2 million seems like an extraordinary event. It's a *shit ton of money*. As the company matures, it begins to feel more real because now the company is actually generating real revenue. I found that I had to be reminded, as dollar values got larger, of my original fuck you number. I lost sight of it, as I did a lot of things. I became wrapped up in the idea of building a "billion-dollar business"—something I never, *ever* cared about previously—and my own sense of money became warped. The investors, the industry rubbed off on me. I'm not proud of it. It's similar to when you start buying designer clothes and forget that it's possible to buy three tank tops for $10. They say as you make more money, the amount you spend in any year expands as well. I have a founder friend who made some money across a few companies. He's got a gorgeous brownstone in Manhattan with a Picasso on the wall, never takes the subway, and always springs for the extra special passes at the concert venue because why not have a private bathroom in the stadium? I love him and it's always a blast hanging, but he embodies this trend: You can afford so much more now, so you do. It's the same with the mental widening that happens with fuck you money. You become enveloped in the promise of the future as opposed to the net present value of the dollar.

This infatuation of future earnings comes back to bite founders in early exit opportunities, as we'll see in a bit. It came back to bite me. I was able to sell some stock during one fundraise. The amount seemed small to me. A friend I had known since I was eighteen reminded me that I had hit my fuck you number and my jaw dropped. She was right. Not only had I forgotten, I had lost my way completely.

The same dissociation with large amounts of money also came up with another founder friend who was fired from his company (by his Seed investors, no less). And as is the tale in most of these cases, post-termination, his company was run by two separate CEOs and not particularly well, and ultimately sold for far less and much later than it should have been. He came away with tens of millions of dollars, though, and over a coffee recently, he shared the psychology that the decade-long process left with him. He had started the company to help fellow IT worker bees like himself do their job more easily. At some point he stopped thinking of himself as one of these worker bees and instead as more like the venture capitalists that sat on his board. After he was fired, he realized he was actually never a part of that rarefied group. Something about the years spent being exposed to **decacorns** and IPOs and seeing wires for millions of dollars warped his sense of self. What was he then, if not the original worker bee he started out helping, nor one of the VCs? He was the VC's worker bee. He's still processing this realization, years later. Money warps, and especially identity.

It is *totally okay* to want to make a few million dollars and be done (so long as you don't tell any investors because they'll never, ever give you a penny). It's different for every founder because the reasons for starting our companies differ. I started my first company because I felt deeply about building a better, more personalized advertising experience and knew that our widget was the best. My second company was started because I wanted to do better than the first. Your reason might be to save the planet or buy your aging parents a house. It doesn't matter what it is; it just matters that you don't lose sight of it. The moment you do, your soul has shed something important.

There *is* a moment between Seed and Series A where a well-run company may very well have at least one offer. It could be an **acquihire**, or it might even be something like $50 million. At that point, assuming you've sold 20% on each of the past two rounds, founders should still collectively own 60%, more or less, of the company. An exit of that size means that each of a pair of founders makes $15 million; of a threesome, $10 million. A solo founder gets the full $30 million. Here we are, on our path to Series A, and we have an offer that will make far more than the fuck you money you started out wanting. What does your brain do? It rejects it. It thinks, "Whoa . . . if someone's offering us this now, what could it be next year?" Your Seed partner will say, "Do you really want to do this? Let's consider our options," and will gently guide you to the logical conclusion of saying no.

There are, of course, many reasons to say no. Odds of a deal going through on limited revenue attainment and this early on is low. Deals have gone awry for far less. You've never run a process like this before. You'll get distracted, the business will start to slip, and the **nonbinding LOI** will disappear. Your competitors will get wind and use it against you (especially if your competition is *the* incumbent trying to buy you).

There's also the strong possibility that this money comes in the form of an earnout (years of hitting targets and signing up to be an indentured servant in order to attain, and even then, not anywhere close because you've lost all leverage). Or the offer comes at the expense of your investors, and the acquirer uses large numbers to make you believe your reputation doesn't matter and you can screw over those who supported you earlier to get this money. It might also be in the form of the buyer's stock and you're trading stock in something you control for stock in something you don't, not to mention zero insight to any board-level goings on.

I once had an offer for $50 million. It required us to cash our investors out (capital in, capital returned) and then the rest would go to the common stock, namely in the form of earnouts. So it wasn't really $50 million; it was pay back the investors, screw over those relationships, and then be a hired gun for the next four years. And that doesn't even include escrow (in which 10% to 15% is held back for a year and you can count on never seeing it). The conversation among the founders was hard. The offer hit one fuck you number but not another. It's moments like these when being a founder duo is hard (50/50 split, you must agree) and being a threesome is impossible (33/33/33 split, two against one wins and then forever you deal with the lingering feelings).

In addition to seeing the opinions on money splinter the team (for possibly the first time), you also start to see people's character revealed. If you, the founder, are willing to screw over an investor to get your fuck you money, what does that say about you? It's selfish to the max. Do you really want to be that person?

There's a movie from 1991 called *Defending Your Life*. In it, humans unlock new lives and new levels of consciousness by being favorably judged when they die. Your life is summed up and adjudicated as to whether you should repeat our world or move onto the next one based on how you behaved. Meryl Streep saves animals from a burning building and Albert Brooks operates in fear. You already know how this love story ends. In hindsight, is screwing over someone who gave you money to execute on your dream something you'd feel good about, or do you live your life like Meryl Streep and keep your eye on the prize? You may choose to do it after an investor crosses you, but starting there seems, well, wrong.

Now, there is something to be said in these moments about staring at your progress, at the market, at your co-founders, and your own mental fatigue so many years into the business with a hypercritical eye. Sometimes it's just time to sell, and I'd argue the founder is best positioned to know when they're too tired to continue or when the winds have changed. But as someone who has been there, tired beyond belief, it feels like giving up. I used to wonder if I could live with myself for stopping simply because I was so tired, especially in light of an up market. We may embrace our society's newfound trend of "it's okay to not be okay," but it still feels crappy to say it out loud. Admitting weakness still isn't mainstream. And it's perhaps hardest to broach the conversation with investors who might still believe in a future outcome that they perceive could be higher. This may be why Jerry's founder chose not to talk about shutting down.

In any case, an offer at this stage is fantastic. Founders get out with large-to-them money and investors get paid back 3x or more. Investors will always try to convince you otherwise (every company is being pushed to be the fund returner). They can do it gently (painting a picture of the fact that if you can get this offer, you can raise money at that number) or aggressively (not hesitating to block a deal). Most likely they won't say no, though, because at this stage you have only Seed money and there is strong reputational risk to the VC to block founders early.

INVESTOR VIEW: FIND FOUNDERS THAT WILL GO BIG

One of the questions I always ask founders before I invest is, "What do you hope the company will look like in five years? In ten years?" I'm not actually trying to find out what the company will look like in five or ten years, I'm trying to find out how ambitious they are. I want to get them on record saying something really ambitious: that their goal is to build a huge company and take it public. That way I can hold them to it later.

Take Liz's example, where the founders own 60% and the investors 40%. There's an offer to buy the company for $50 million. The founders would get $30 million and the investors $20 million. The founders walk away with life-changing money! The investors do not. The VC firm earns a couple million dollars. This is a lot of money, even after being split between the partners and though it is earned over four years. But this kind of return isn't a great success for a VC. It doesn't "return the fund," and given the high risk that the company could have failed, the VCs would have been better off putting the money in the stock market. That would have been less work, too.

CARRY: THE BIG MONEY

An aside on that couple of million dollars: When a VC raises a fund from LPs, the usual deal is that the VC gets paid (1) a management fee—akin to the fee you might pay your mutual fund manager, usually, in the VC case, 2% of the money invested per year—and (2) a carry, usually calculated as 20% of the investment profits. If the VC turns a $100 million fund into $300 million of value, they get paid a carry of 20% of the $200 million profit, or $40 million.

So, in Liz's example, if the VC invested $10 million and got back $20 million the carry would be $2 million. Successful VCs make most of their compensation in carry. Carry creates an incentive for the VC to make as much as possible for their investors, but it also can create a "swing for the fences" mentality because the VC shares in gains but not losses.

Because of the power law, no VC can build their business—much less their reputation—on small exits. What is small? Anything that doesn't return the fund. Because, remember, one company returns it, but no one knows which one. Exiting early takes one of the VC's opportunities off the table.

I understand the desire to get out. And it's not just about the money. For me, when I was a founder, the interesting part was getting the company from zero to one; managing a big enterprise was not my thing. Plus, it was wreaking havoc on my personal life—running a startup is all-consuming, there is always more that needs to be done. Selling the company felt like the perfect solution, but we had sold our investors on a bigger vision.

As an investor I want my founders to feel the same way: When they asked me for money, they said they wanted to go the distance, and I'd like them to keep their word. Nine out of ten of the biggest venture-backed exits are IPOs. I look for founders who believe they can manage their company while it is a scrappy startup, when it is a larger private company, and when it is a big public company. If they don't believe they can, they'll be tempted to sell too soon.

In the Fundraising chapter, I said I want to know a founder's ambitions, and this is why. If they're going to fold early, I'd just as soon not get involved.

FOUNDER VIEW: CO-FOUNDER ALIGNMENT IN PIVOTAL MOMENTS

Let's assume Jerry has gotten into your head and you decide to reject this early offer. You're going bigger and that means more money and it comes time to raise a Series A. This means you're working for that triple-triple-double-double (which so few companies ever actually hit, and that, combined with the fact that there are *so* many other ways that companies grow successfully, means that *the* yardstick for success is demoralizing from the onset). Your investors now have an exit threshold written into the docs. If your valuation on the A was $50 million, that threshold now might be $150 million. It means investors are guaranteed a 3x return and they still have a right to block the deal. They can block the deal anyway (out of spite, because they want more money, because they can), but the new funding now provides a tangible data point.

Exits from this point on are going to be at least $250 million. You're in a whole new game, and the politics reviewed in the Board of Directors chapter start to become critical. Real money is at stake. The opportunity for an offer diminishes simply because the number of suitors diminishes, and also because they are larger and so move more slowly. If there were five hundred companies who'd consider buying you at $50 million, there are twenty-five at $250 million, maybe five at $1 to $5 billion, and then your only choice is to IPO. Those early offers become attractive when looking back. Very attractive. That fuck you number you ignored for the next step . . . it's really quite beautiful when you get tired.

It's critical to consider two more issues before turning down an offer:

1. How tired are we as founders? Is one of us more tired than another?

2. If we disagree with each other, is saying no going to cause a rift that we can't overcome personally (and thus operationally)?

These are actually the same question. If the founders don't agree on a life decision such as this (because let's be clear, we are talking about *millions of dollars*), what happens to the team?

At one company, we had been at it for five years before we got our first real verbal offer: one year of ideating, one year of running down a business we ultimately scrapped, and three more years of building and selling. We were tired. One of us was more tired and had a more mature family situation. This person also hadn't had any real financial success after decades of working in startups. They wanted out and their fuck you number was in front of them.

The idea of screwing over the investors wasn't appealing to the rest of us. We didn't believe we'd be able to raise money again after that and we both wanted to start companies again (selfishness masquerading as character, actually). The decision came down to (1) what was "right," and (2) money (only one had hit their fuck you number).

We said no. And it for sure caused a rift in an otherwise healthy dynamic. This was the first of the arguments that could have torn us apart, and they were all pretty fundamental to the business. The first was killing the original product and pivoting. The second was getting into Y Combinator and turning it down. The third was this acquisition question and it took some months before we felt back to normal as a founding team. The fourth was pausing product development for a few months to shore up our ability to deliver what we said we were going to. The list goes on and on.

EGO ABOUNDS, EVEN IN INCUBATORS

This is one of my favorite stories, so permit me a non sequitur. We turned Y Combinator down for a series of reasons: didn't like the legal language, didn't like the fact that they essentially had the rights to transfer our stock without our approval to any entity, didn't ultimately believe we needed the cachet that went with their imprimatur, were worried we wouldn't get sufficient attention in their large class size. When I got on the phone to say thank you but no thank you, one of the partners proceeded to tell me that nobody who had ever turned YC down had gone on to be worth a billion dollars and, "There are no outcomes between zero and a billion dollars," to which I responded, "I believe there are nine hundred ninety-nine million," and then he hung up on me.

If you're doing things right, you'll typically be in alignment with your co-founders and *want* to be in alignment with your co-founders. These people are your partners. But this handful of moments will be hard, none harder than exit opportunities. These decisions will be excruciating to make. Your startup is your life. It's not your business; it's your life. And it's your co-founders' lives too, which are different from your own. And herein of course again lies the tension with investors: Your life is your investor's *business*.

INVESTOR VIEW: DON'T SELL TOO SOON

Investors really want one thing, and one thing only: to have invested in blockbuster, return-the-fund companies. That can't happen if they exit too early.

Here's my advice on exiting, to both founders and investors: Don't even think about it, until you absolutely have to. Successful businesses grow exponentially for a while, and the longer a company can ride that **hockey stick**, the bigger and more important the company gets, and the more money everyone makes.

If you look at the chart, you can see what I mean. This is a company I invested in, The Trade Desk. The chart shows their revenue from inception until IPO, and their valuation at each round.[1] Revenue grew exponentially, and so did the valuation. The founder CEO owned 23% of the company after the IPO, worth about $600 million. If he had sold earlier, say in 2011, he would have certainly made less than $10 million. Waiting paid. (In fact, the company has done quite well since the IPO as well, and the founder still owns a large chunk of his shares, so he has done even better.)

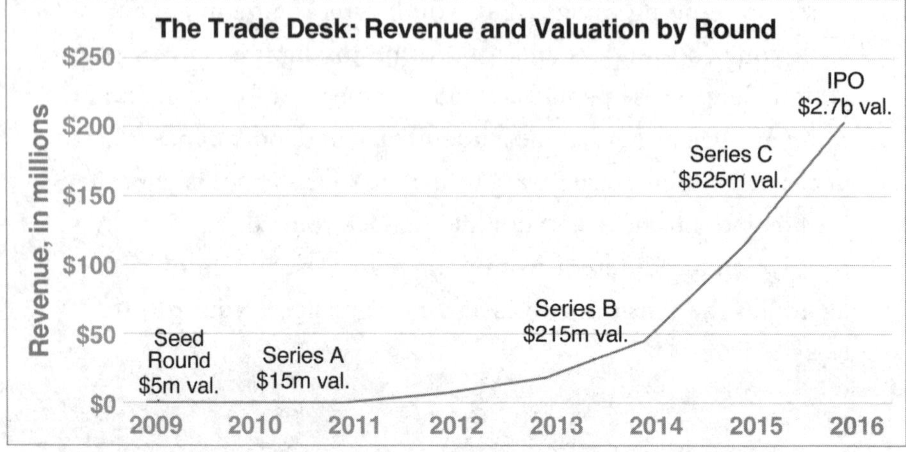

When the exit does come, the best case is an IPO. IPOs almost always offer the highest valuation available. You can see, in The Trade Desk chart, that the private valuation, the Series C in March of 2016, was one-fifth the IPO valuation, just six months later. It's the **greater fool theory** in action. After that, from best to worst:

1. Some big company comes in out of the blue with a huge offer.
2. The company realizes it is at an inflection point in its valuation and solicits an acquisition offer.
3. The founder loses their nerve and decides to exit early.
4. The company is not working, can't raise money, and has to sell before they fail.
5. The company can't find a buyer and has to lay everyone off and shut the doors.

The third option—losing their nerve—is the most disappointing, because it's the biggest missed opportunity. Sometimes things just don't work, but having someone decide they'd rather sell before that happens is uniquely painful. If it was the founder's idea, the investors might lose faith in them.

LOSING FAITH

A founder I worked with got an offer to buy his company. It was a good offer, but not great. He brought it to the board and suggested they might want to take it. The board mulled it over for a couple of weeks and then fired him. He apparently "didn't believe in the business strongly enough." The company went on for another couple of years and then was sold for parts. The investors lost almost all their money. But they still felt they had made the right gamble. Maybe they had.

Sometimes the next-to-worst option—selling before they fail—feels great, because it's like dodging a bullet. You might not make money, but at least you didn't lose it all.

DODGING A BULLET

I was an investor in a company that was doing well and raising a round. In the midst of the process, the CTO decided he couldn't take the constant changes in product direction anymore (he didn't really belong at a startup). He found another job and gave the CEO two days' notice. Now the CEO was stuck: No one would invest without a CTO, and no qualified CTO would join a company about to run out of money. The CEO reached out to some large tech companies that could use the technology he developed, explained that he needed to sell quickly and was flexible on price, and managed to get one interested enough to buy his company.

I didn't make money on that investment, but I didn't lose any either. The CEO went on to become an executive at the buyer. While I still wish we could have seen what his company could have become, neither of us can complain about the outcome, given the circumstances. I got to **recycle** the money into another startup and he ended up in a great job, so we both got another shot at success.

If the founder decides to sell, and the board agrees, there's a right way to go about it and a wrong way. The old saw in the venture world is that companies aren't sold; they're bought. Nobody wants to sell life insurance to someone who comes looking for it. Similarly, no one wants to buy a company from someone who wants to sell. Given this, the best way to sell a company is for the founder to convince someone else they really want to buy it even though the company doesn't really want to sell.

It's easy to convince someone else they want to buy a company that has an excellent product, fast-growing revenue, and an amazing team of people. If the startup poses an existential competitive threat to the potential buyer, that's a bonus; the easiest way for a big tech company to respond to a competitive threat is to buy them. If a startup is in this position, though, usually no one, especially the investors, will want to sell. Exceptions include some hidden problem—management team issues, perhaps—or something extrinsic, ranging from a bigger company implicitly threatening ruinous competition to the lead VC's fund reaching the end of its ten-year life.

Alternatively, if the startup is out raising capital and is worried about whether they'll be able to or not, they can approach companies who might be potential buyers, but ask them to be a **strategic** investor in the round. This gives the startup an opportunity to tell their most optimistic story, where they become so successful they overtake all the incumbents. Needless to say, these incumbents include the potential buyer the story is being told to. Fear of this might convince them not to fund the startup but to buy it.

ASKING FOR INVESTMENT, GETTING ACQUIRED

One founder I worked with was having a hard time raising his company's Series C round and approached a much bigger company in his market. He told them how fast the company was growing, that it had a potential term sheet for a $75 million pre-money, and asked if they would like to be a small investor in the syndicate. Of course, he couldn't offer them a board seat because of competitive concerns, but it would be a very good investment. The bigger company couldn't have cared less about investment returns (public companies don't get any credit in the stock market for one-time investment returns, or one-time anything, really) but after buying into the story—and seeing how some big-name VCs had bought into the story—they started to believe that owning the company could make *them* the innovative new player in the market instead of this startup. Within a week they had proffered an "unsolicited" term sheet to buy the company for $75 million.

The founder, who had nerves of steel, immediately called them back and said his VC backers would not go for it . . . they wanted to *buy* equity at $75 million, not sell it. The next day the buyer doubled their offer. The board—grudgingly, in public; gleefully, in private—accepted it.

Even when the company isn't looking to sell, potential "acquirers" pop up all the time. Most of them are not serious; they're either fishing for information or trawling the market. But if they aren't just tourists, their interest can be leveraged into an offer, and then the board needs to decide if they want to sell at that price. I said that investors would generally prefer to wait, but sometimes an offer is so good they decide to sell.

TAKE YOUR OPPORTUNITIES

Cruise Automation, a self-driving car company, was founded in October 2013. The company raised about $19 million in venture capital before General Motors stepped in to buy them in March 2016, when the company was only two and a half years old. GM paid, depending on who you believe, somewhere between $580 million and $1 billion for Cruise. It would have been understandable if Cruise had decided, like the founders of Google had, to keep building, in search of a much larger exit down the road. But in retrospect, 2016 was the peak of the self-driving car mania, so they sold at exactly the right time.

FOUNDER VIEW: IT'S WICKED HARD TO FIND A BUYER

Companies *are* bought, not sold. So let's talk about how to architect a sale.

First, it doesn't make sense to ignore acquirers until you need them. I've tried to sell my companies three separate times, and in every instance, I was utterly stymied by not having relationships in place. If the investors you have today struggle to introduce you to investors or prospects or executives, they're going to do even worse introducing you to potential acquirers. And the most likely acquirers are the ones who really want you gone from the market one way or another, so you are probably avoiding them by design.

In hindsight, I should have been cultivating all potential buyers, and specifically the right people at the company (but I also had that time-consuming day job of being CEO). The right person is never **Corp Dev** (the team that executes acquisitions). You might think they are, but like CISOs and consultants, these teams have no power. You'll instead have to make your case to someone with actual decision-making authority, typically a leader in a revenue-generating function, such as the head of product or even the CEO themselves. The challenge with telling a compelling story for acquisition is that these relationships take years to build. And it's not just with one person, but with a whole set of people in multiple parts of a company that all carry serious decision-making or decision-killing power.

You need these relationships to be strong and in place before you get to the point of putting them to use, because you might need them to force their organization to move much more quickly than it's used to. Investors are old pros at putting down term sheets quickly; acquirers: not so much. If you're competing with them, they're old and stodgy and move like molasses.

The last time I ran a sales process parallel to a fundraise, one of the companies with whom we spoke instead offered to invest. When I said, "Great, let's get you added to the round!" they responded that it would take them six months to get through their diligence. This was a public company with a $6 billion market cap and it was going to take them *six months* to decide on investing a few million dollars. Imagine what a sale would have looked like! We said no thank you and moved on with life.

The question becomes, how do you get relevant companies to give you the time of day before you're at the acquisition point? Your company is young. The product is young and immature. Why would they want to speak to you? The only reason is to get a closer look at what you're doing, which might be exactly what you don't want.

Perhaps that instinct is wrong. I used to feel the same way, but as your company gets bigger, competitors naturally became frenemies or even partners and then it becomes obvious: It's an eventuality that a company that might want to acquire us also might have a reason to have a relationship with us. My thought process here began maturing, and I began to think more about sharing what we were working on *for this reason and this reason alone*. Some large company problems lie in the fact that they can't build quickly anymore. I realized it wasn't the worst thing to impress them with what we had built. If anything, it might light enough of a fire for them to want to acquire us! Certainly they couldn't compete. They'd have to partner. Or buy.

This gets you some optionality, but these relationships must already be in place and that often takes years. How else could a busy founder CEO do that when they haven't been focusing on it?

Well, there's at least one other option, but only for companies at a maturing revenue stage (let's say on a clear path to $5 million ARR). Imagine you're a big incumbent and suddenly a $250,000 ARR marquee deal gets won by a startup. One of your AEs then misses quota. It doesn't get escalated to the CRO, but they lose two more deals in six months and *that* makes it up to management. If you can be the startup that turns into the gnat that turns into the wasp, you've just created yourself a market.

Next, you need a trigger like a term sheet with a drop-dead date. Without a forcing function, you have no control, unless you're the hottest startup on the market (a rare joy indeed) or can stone-cold bluff.

Now, let's assume you've proven value and there's a trigger, and they want to buy you. They'll issue an LOI. It's going to be non-binding and that **breakup clause** still may not be enough for them to complete the deal. And then there's an earnout and some percentage of both compensation and escrow that you'll actually never get and then there are the internal politics of the new organization, not the least of which is your own misery as a hired gun working for someone else, in control of nothing. Ugh. But at least it's done, right?

There's another way to sell your company: using your investors. The best of them know everyone and can get you in touch quickly with the right folks with actual power and authority at an acquirer. Getting their help, however, requires you being more or less open with them about selling the company, which is a huge can of worms, and then whatever you say to the person to whom you're introduced will get right back to your investor.

An investor also might choose to introduce you to acquirers for their own sundry reasons. I once had one attempt to do it because they wanted to divest themselves of the asset. They placed a call to a company where they had a board seat; a verbal offer emerged. It was filled with caveats: many tens of millions less than the market said we were worth, it was going to take six months to complete, it was nonbinding, there was additional diligence to do, the company had just spent a large amount of money the year prior on another acquisition that hadn't yet been integrated, the CEO really didn't want to do it, and so on and so forth. The offer was a joke. At the same time, it did showcase for me the true power of some rare VCs who can pick up the phone and get something done.

As I write this, I honestly do wonder how companies ever sell themselves. They all seem to fail in some way. The biggest companies seem to continue to be run independently (MSFT/GitHub,

Google/YouTube, IBM/Red Hat) or go belly-up (Yahoo!/Tumblr, Walmart/Jet), the ones worth "only" a few billion seem to end up stalling (Okta/Auth0), and smallish ones end up going belly-up (either bought to absorb a failing competitor, in which case the competitor hates the acquirer and everything fails, or it just fails on execution), and the tiny ones are acquihires and nothing else. Perhaps it really is IPO or bust.

INVESTOR VIEW: COMPANIES COME AND GO, BUT FOUNDER RELATIONSHIPS SHOULD BE FOREVER

Any exit other than an IPO is stressful. They can strain the investor-founder dynamic like no other situation. There's bound to be differences of opinion about how much the company should sell for. And there are often some differences of opinion about who should get the money. Even though it seems like this should be clearly spelled out in the contracts, it's amazing how quickly some people can forget what they agreed to when it's time to divvy up the spoils.

We talked about founders and investors having goals besides money in Fear, Trust, and Making Money, but when the company is exiting, those other goals become moot. Management will probably change after the acquisition, the vision will change, the partnership between VC and founder will be over, solving the customers' problems becomes someone else's task, and any dreams of working together toward an even bigger outcome are done. The only thing left to fight about is the money.

But relationships endure from this startup to the next one. These relationships are valuable. A good relationship might benefit you in the exit itself, if the founder has to make choices about who gets certain perks, for example.

IT'S NOT ALWAYS ABOUT THE MONEY

In one case, a company I'd invested in was raising a venture round when a strategic popped up and offered to acquire the company for a very good price. The company agreed and they started the process. The founders soon realized the acquirer was slow-walking the contract and due diligence processes. The company was short on cash (that's why they were looking for another round of financing in the first place) and the strategic probably figured that if they ran out the clock, they would be able to force the company into accepting a lower offer.

To keep from being squeezed, the company asked its major investors to lend them money until the sale process was completed. One of the major investors, realizing the company was over a barrel, said they would lend the money but only on onerous terms (essentially, the loan would have to be repaid at two times the amount put in, even though it would be outstanding only until the acquisition was complete, no more than a couple of months). With no other options, the founders took the deal.

This sounds pretty harsh on the founders, and it was. The founders put as much of their personal funds in as they could afford. I offered to lend them some money personally so they could buy more of the note, and charge only nominal interest, but the loan was, in fact, at least moderately risky and the founders did not want to end up not being able to repay me. They instead set aside a piece of the note for me to invest in. This was the only time in my career an investment paid more than 200% annualized, even if it was for only a few months.

> It may sound dumb to lend money to the founders when I could invest myself and make much more, but I had built a relationship with these founders over many years. They were friends. It also paid off when one of them started their next company: I was the first person they approached to invest.

The relationship might also matter if the company is being acquired by another private company and you don't have access to the acquiring company's financials (this isn't unusual; the board of the company being sold will have access, but the buyer might not want every investor to see sensitive info). Sometimes you have the choice of selling your equity for either cash or stock (or something weird, like an earnout) in the combined business. If you don't know how the acquiring company is doing, you can't make an informed choice. The founder will have the info, and the informal inside scoop. They are under NDA, but if they trust you and like you, they may help you figure out what the better deal is. If you think the acquiring company is on their way to greatness, you might decide to roll over your investment into the new company.

When a company's exit is the involuntary kind—when the business is just not working—sometimes it's because the company's timing just wasn't right. Everything else—founders, team, product—was great, but the company still didn't work. Maybe customers weren't ready to adopt the product, maybe partners couldn't prioritize it just then, maybe some unpredictable macro-economic event ruined the market. In these cases, you want to be there when the founder starts their next company. If you were there for the founder when things weren't going right and didn't fly off the handle because you were losing some money (which is nothing compared to the founder losing their company), the founder will call you back next time they raise. I have been included in highly contested Seed rounds next to legendary VC firms because the founder insisted I get a piece. When Liz started her second company, she included me from the beginning. While I lost all my money on her first company (the company that bought hers ended up failing), it looks like I'll make it back on her second. In general, founders pick VCs based on their reputations. If you do the right things, people notice and opportunities follow.

FOUNDER VIEW: THE BEST WAY TO ACTUALLY MAKE MONEY

The tension between VCs and founders vis-à-vis exits is based solely on timing and ownership. The earlier in the company's lifecycle, the more money the founders will make and the easier it is for them to exit. At a Seed stage, founders most likely still control the board and the investor probably won't risk their reputation and exercise blocking rights. As companies hit Series B and beyond, founder control is lost (or fear of investors is at least strongly at play for some founders), and those minimum exit value thresholds in the IRA are aggressively fought over during the round. Investors won't hesitate to tell the founders no if they see massive multiples in their future. Remember, investors will risk your whole company to return the fund; you still need to make your mortgage payments.

It's possible that the best way to mitigate risk while waiting for an exit that may never materialize is the co-sale exemption discussed in the Terms chapter.

Now, investors *can* get nasty and not approve the round if they feel you don't deserve the money. Yes, I said "deserve," and yes, that means sometimes the whims of later-stage investors (who've made so much money that nothing matters anymore except the game) control the founders' financial future vs. predicating decisions on actual merit. When an investor's biggest problem is that his wife is angry that he is going to buy another yacht and that's all he'll talk about over lunch, know that you are nothing and will be at the mercy of his whims. Some investors *do* recognize that exits take more than a decade and if the founders are doing a good enough job, there's no reason to alienate them by fighting this request. The act of taking money off the table can diffuse the financial anxiety that comes with going for the giant exit. Big time. I've seen it firsthand.

Where does this leave us? I think I've convinced myself exits are a waste of everyone's time in every possible way—getting them into a position of possibility, doing the deal, living with the deal—except it's one of only three ways out. You fail, you get acquired (most often acquihired), or you IPO. The journey to an acquisition is fraught with politics and implications and money and is Disaster Incarnate when it comes to the founder/investor relationship, not to mention the suffering of the employees who truly care, who are also going through these ups and downs right next to you. I think I now believe that there are actually only two options: IPO or bust. And perhaps the best option for a founder is to make their millions in co-sale rights, in perpetuity. Or maybe I should just become an investor.

KEY TAKEAWAYS

FOUNDER	INVESTOR
Co-founders need to remember why they started the company and ensure they're on the same page with each other.	Because exits are the last chance for VCs to influence the outcome of their investment, they can be especially contentious.
Money changes people. Know what amount of money constitutes success for you and stick to it.	Investors look for founders that want to go big, and pressure founders not to bail early.
Exits are harder to come as the company gets later-stage.	The best returns come when a growing company stays private as long as possible. The best way to exit is usually an IPO. Next best is a sale to another company.
Exits are always hard and require years of cultivating relationships *or* flawless execution.	Selling to another company requires careful planning to maximize the value.
Because exits can take a long time, founders can and should take money off the table to mitigate risk. VCs generally aren't supportive and this will ruin their chances at teaming up with the founder again.	Sometimes the most fruitful collaboration with a founder is the company after the current one. VCs must be supportive of founder goals and needs, to a point, if they hope to work together again in the future.

7

RED AND THE WOLF

Jerry: Hey, Liz.

Liz: Hi, Jerry!

Jerry: So now that we've put all the things we've argued about for years down on paper, do you feel better or worse about the whole VC/founder relationship?

Liz: I feel less emotional about it for sure. The process solidified the fact that a business is a business irrespective of whether or not it's mine, and that fact comes with implications. You?

Jerry: It's made me realize that the difference between what VCs feel like they need to do and what founders think VCs plan to do is pretty stark. I think this book is worthwhile if only because people should know that.

Liz: I recently got a bit of a desperate call from two founders who built an absolutely beautiful product and are just beginning to sell it. One of their earliest investors told them they were doing a bad job. I don't think that it ever occurred to them that they might encounter criticism that wasn't necessarily warranted nor asked for nor on point. They didn't have the tools to manage either the investor or their own reaction, both of which were unexpected to them. There are a series of things that the founder doesn't know they're going to encounter in running the company. In this case it was unsolicited, mentally harmful advice. I was sad that they were so taken aback.

Jerry: I think there are a lot of things that founders don't expect, but also things they do expect but that aren't going to happen. Before I invest, I tell founders I can be helpful in very specific ways. I can be helpful in raising more money, but I can't be helpful in introducing you to customers, for example. But a few months later, after telling this to my founders, they'll come back and say, hey, can you introduce me to customers? They ask for the things that I said I couldn't do.

The founder needs to discern that different people are good at different things. VCs may say, "I'm really good at everything and I can help you with all this stuff," but in reality, they can't. They aren't generalists. Venture capital is a business of extremes. Maybe this book will help founders pick their VCs more intentionally.

Liz: VCs aren't going to want founders to hear that. After this book is released, I suspect I'll still be able to raise money again. But for the investor, if you're saying shit's fucked up, I suspect it might hurt your reputation.

Jerry: Are you saying you won't take my money anymore?

When I wrote the blog post that inspired this book, I got pushback from other investors who said it wasn't true. They said, "This is not what we do," even though I know it is because I've seen them work. They also said, "This isn't what we want founders to think of us."

They want founders to focus on what's going to happen in the best case, not when things go badly. Everything's all carrot until the founder gets the term sheet and sees the stick. Then they're forced to think about all the possible bad things for the first time and at the last minute.

Liz: And sometimes they don't think about it until they actually get to the docs themselves. Why do you think it is that founders don't consider the downside of taking venture money themselves before this point?

Jerry: Because the downside of venture money is theoretical and probably years in the future. Running out of money is today. Also, I think everyone's on their best behavior during the courtship, but then at the wedding, the VC whips out the prenup. You have to take it or leave it, with not a lot of time to think about it.

Liz: If I had a hope for this book, it would be that a founder says, "I'm going to go and diligence every investor." I wish founders back channeled as soon as they possibly could. Get off the phone with an investor and immediately call around and ask, "What don't I know?"

Jerry: Investors do that with founders all the time and I absolutely agree that's what founders should do with investors. The other thing that investors try to do is to get to know somebody over time. If you deal with somebody for a couple of months, you'll see these things happening because you're interacting with them.

It should be a much more cold-blooded calculus. Do you need this money or not? And if you absolutely do, then is this the right person to work with, and are they offering fair terms? The cash and the venture capitalist come as a package.

Liz: And then there's the running of the company itself. There's money and then there's operations and governance. The conflict comes down to the difference between the two. What is the right thing for the business as opposed to what is the thing that the person who gave me money is telling me to do? They are completely and utterly distinct. I think that's what venture capital gets wrong. I almost wish you could abstract the founder and the VC out of the governance portion of the company itself.

Jerry: That's the core of the conflict, I think. Founders want the money to do what they think is right and they also don't want anyone telling them what to do. But investors need to be able to course-correct how their money is being spent.

Liz: I agree with that perspective. And while I love the idea of having infinite latitude, I need a shit ton of help in order to get anything over the finish line and I alone am insufficient. Investors can and do provide help in many ways.

Jerry: I feel like when I say "course-correct," you hear "help the founder do what they want to do." That's not really what I mean at all. It often means "tell the founder to do something different." The VCs aren't there to help *you*.

Liz: I couldn't disagree more. Anybody who is involved in my company works for me. That holds whether you're an employee or an investor. You now work with me in an effort to get this thing big and over whatever the proverbial finish line is. And every VC who has signed up to invest in my company knows that they work for me. I send email after email after email soliciting help.

Jerry: And yet in the real world, when somebody pays you money, you work for them. That's what they get in return for their money.

Liz: Are you trying to be purposely provocative?

Jerry: Aren't you?

VC governance is on the front pages again because of the FTX bankruptcy, and venture capitalists are being blamed for not doing enough diligence beforehand, not providing oversight as the company went off the rails. They got the same criticism for Theranos with an amazing idea that turned out to not be doable, although those weren't professional VCs. And they got the same criticism for WeWork where the founder was spending money in ways that really didn't build the business. How is it that venture capitalists should simultaneously have less oversight or be less involved in telling the founder what to do and, on the other hand, be at fault when they don't?

Liz: Telling a founder what to do and being a good governor of the business are two separate things. Telling a founder what to do is like a founder working for that investor. Spend this money, hire this executive, don't build that feature. Those are pure operational tasks. In that case of FTX, say, if they had looked at the balance sheet, the issue would have become obvious. That's Governance 101.

Jerry: I don't think there's a bright line between one and the other. Do you think there's a way of getting founders and investors on the same page from the beginning so this kind of friction doesn't happen?

Liz: No way. VCs claim to be risk takers, and while that is their business, they simply care too much about covering their asses. I pride myself on honest relationships with all of my investors, often to a fault. I share more instead of less because that's how I want to be treated, and yet when the shit hits the fan, I've learned the hard way that I don't actually know what they're capable of. Nothing matters more to them than their reputation, their returns, and not rocking the boat within their own industry with their peers. I come second to fear and money, no matter how good of a job I'm doing.

Jerry: That's kind of a nihilistic view.

Liz: Venture capital serves a very specific master, which is to help you grow incredibly quickly at a time when, if you do so and you execute well, you will win the market. If you take venture capital, it's only because winning the entire market is better than the downside of never having a shot in the first place.

Jerry: So you would take venture capital again?

Liz: [long pause] If I were to do it again, I'd want to do it differently. I would think about ways to level the playing field like getting rid of preferred stock or attempting to find a way of true governance that neutralizes my emotion, my investors' emotion, and both of our egos.

If you were to start a company now, how would you fund it?

Jerry: I would fund it through venture capital if it was the kind of company that needed to grow very quickly. But I would choose my investors very carefully. Some VCs I've been on boards with did everything right; they were constructive, optimistic, and helpful. They didn't micromanage but listened well, let you know when they disagreed, and suggested alternatives. If I could find those kinds of investors, I would take their money.

Liz: But most are bad, or at best, can't be trusted. They lean out, and when they lean out, they try once or twice to say something and then they go, "Fuck this, I don't need this company anymore, I'm just going to wash my hands of it," or they call you back in a week and you're fired.

If I were an investor, I'd try to do it differently. Say I were recommending a founder hire AEs and the founder said no. Instead of trying to convince them I was right, I'd dig in and ask why. I'd say, "Here are the hallmarks of twenty-five other companies that look just like yours and this is why they chose this moment to hire. Tell me why that doesn't feel accurate." I'd want to figure out where the decision was coming from. If it was an emotional decision, like I'm allergic to sales, that's different from an actual tactical reason as to why sales won't work for the company. I would lean into the conflict.

Jerry: I think there's a middle ground between never-ending conflict and "my way or the highway."

Liz: I'd like to agree and yet, as you know, my experience has often been different. Maybe you should raise a fund and be one of the good ones. You're one of the few I do trust.

Jerry: If I were running other people's money, instead of my own, I would probably feel more pressure to focus on the success of the company and not the success of the founder. I'd also be more heavily involved later in the company's life, so I'd have to react to more concrete problems. I think my advice would have to be less Socratic and more direct. I'm not sure founders would appreciate that.

Liz: Do you think it's always been this way, that founders and investors have been at odds, having not been alive when venture capital started? Sandy Lerner's foreword clearly says yes and I would personally say that seems true.

Jerry: Yeah, I mean, back when I was a kid, Henry Ford got pushed out of his first company. [Liz spits water out of her nose.] His investors pushed him out of the Henry Ford Company. That company became Cadillac. It was his next company that became the Ford we know today. He didn't get along with his investors at Ford either; his backers sued him when they disagreed with his growth plans. There's always been this sort of principal/agent problem between the people who put the money in and insist on some control and the people who get the money but run the company. Whenever founders and investors co-own a company and it's valuable enough for them to fight over, they will. This book's not going to change that.

Liz: No, and this book is, if nothing else, a whole bunch of information on the types of conversations and confrontations that may happen. That might lead you to make different decisions, like saying no to a term sheet simply because you read an anecdote and you're like, "I wonder how this could affect me in this situation." Or consider that you might be best friends with your co-founder today but think about how to protect against them changing seven years down the line. If this book causes either side to slow down and be a little bit more thoughtful, just knowing, that's pretty awesome.

Jerry: There are always going to be disagreements over how to run the company, but if you understand what's driving them, you can make those disagreements part of the process. Maybe those disagreements don't end with the founder getting fired or the company getting sold early, or any of the million other ways a company might not reach its potential. The founder gets to build what they wanted to build and the investor makes more money. Everyone is happy. At least that's the hope.

Liz: I watched *Bullet Train* last night. Probably the worst movie on the planet.

Jerry: Loved that movie.

Liz: Seriously?

Jerry: I like that kind of movie.

Liz: Here we go again. Anyway, in it, a number of times, Brad Pitt says, "Whoa, whoa, whoa. If we're acting from emotion instead of from understanding, everybody loses." If there's one hope that I could have for this book, it's that people slow down and say, "Why is the other person doing this?" before they act.

Jerry: Do you think he's raising? I should reach out.

REFERENCES

CHAPTER 4: THE BOARD OF DIRECTORS

1. Brad Feld and Mahendra Ramsinghani, *Startup Boards: Getting the Most Out of Your Board of Directors* (Wiley, 2013), p. 145.

CHAPTER 5: GROWTH

1. Paul Graham, "Startup = Growth," paulgraham.com, September 2012, https://www.paulgraham.com/growth.html.
2. Okta financials, Crunchbase, https://www.crunchbase.com/organization/okta/company_financials.
3. OneLogin financials, Crunchbase, https://www.crunchbase.com/organization/onelogin/company_financials.
4. Datadog financials, Crunchbase, https://www.crunchbase.com/organization/datadog/company_financials.
5. Loggly financials, Crunchbase, https://www.crunchbase.com/organization/loggly/company_financials.
6. Sriram Krishnan, "Mike Cannon-Brookes," The Observer Effect, October 31 2021, https://theobservereffect.org/mikecannonbrookes.html.

CHAPTER 6: EXITS

1. This chart was made entirely from publicly available information: Crunchbase and TTD's SEC filings. The numbers are estimates.

JOINT ACKNOWLEDGMENTS

The authors would like to thank Tim Burgard of HarperCollins for believing this book truly was something different, and Alice Martell for showing us newbies how things were done.

It is our honor to have Sandy Lerner pen the foreword to this book. We are indebted to you.

Thanks to Noelle Thurlow, Noah Pepper, Josh Reich, Owen Davis, Jonathan Hirschman, Susan Lawler, John Lawler, Justin Singer, Nick Ducoff, Laura Nooney, Andy Magnusson, Aneel Lakhani, Drew Blas, Melanie Rubenstein, Benjamin Shamash, Britt Crawford, Scott Bessler, Matt Witheiler, Jonathan Zalman, Eric Steinhardt, Gary Goldberg, Greg Yardley, Vaughn Tan, Jake Stein, Mary Mazza, Marty McCall, and Baochi Nguyen for reading and editing for hours and hours and hours until the prose sang.

Thanks to Olly Farshi for taking epic photos, and Daisy Press for coaching our voices into liquid gold.

A special thanks to Marty McCall and Baochi Nguyen for helping launch this startup.

FOUNDER'S NOTE

I wrote v1 of this book during a time of great turmoil. The words poured out, mostly within a three-week span. I found the act cathartic. You may find some rhetoric to be charged, provocative, perhaps angry at times. These feelings were certainly present while writing, although I do hope the editing makes the vitriol as digestible as possible.

You may also come away thinking that I dislike everyone and the industry as a whole. That would be wrong. My co-author is one of my closest friends and he funds companies for a living.

It is also true that investors in this industry have hurt me and other founders in staggering ways. VCs are in the business of making money (or letting their egos get the better of them), and that frequently comes at the cost of founders. I'm surprised I haven't heard of a founder committing suicide.

This book was written in the hopes of leveling the playing field. Information is power, and, at a minimum, this story will be eye-opening for the founder. And that is who I aim to serve, because you are me.

As a founder, my highs have been crazy high and my lows insanely low. Daily life is boring after a startup. It's a mindfuck to build a company, and the job is *really* hard to do without true friends. And sometimes those true friends you started out with . . . well, they change. Painfully, yes, often heinously so. This book *is* the friend I wish I'd had and the one I hope you'll turn to in times of need.

Can you trust me? I suppose that's the question. For the first time in my career, I answer to nobody but myself. I'm also no angel, as you'll read. And Jerry cares about a lot, but not what others in the venture community think of him.

Thanks to my co-author, Jerry, for being one of the best people I know and finding a way to work *with* someone for the first time in twenty years.

Thanks again to Sandy Lerner for taking a leap of faith on a stranger. You are wickedly subversive and I am grateful for your friendship.

And personal thanks to Jon, Nick, Ben, David, Jenna, girl Sandy, boy Sandy, Stacey, Uncle Lenny, Eric, Brian Noe, Brian Gryn, Jeffrey, Laurence, Brandi, Roy, Yair, Melly, Aneel, Ida, Dad, and every friend, employee, early investor, and customer of strongDM. If you picked up the phone anytime I called in the past fifteen years and listened to me cry, know that I am forever in your debt. Thank you.

INVESTOR'S NOTE

This book isn't new knowledge. No one who has been in the startup world for more than a few years will think, "Gee golly, I didn't know that." It's just knowledge that no one likes to say out loud. All of us have an interest in making sure innovators can start companies, run them well, and make some money doing it. It's how the world gets changed, mostly for the better. That's the three steps forward; this book is about avoiding the two steps back.

We tell the outside world that founders and investors are always rational, competent, and willing to work together for what is best. In reality, our industry has both the brutal politics of high-stakes businesses and the petty politics of low-stakes realms. Pretending this isn't so hasn't really helped anyone. Maybe telling it like it is will.

The post that inspired this book stemmed from the same turmoil that Liz was going through. Which just goes to show that, despite this book being about conflicts between founders and investors, in the twelve-plus years we have worked together, we have always managed to work them out. I'm her biggest fan. I suspect many VCs are the biggest fans of many of the founders they underwrite. This doesn't, of course, change the underlying calculus of the job. That's also what the book is about.

When she suggested writing this book, I had to figure out how to balance it with my full-time job (investing), my part-time job (teaching), and my family. Investing is merciless, but thank you to Columbia for letting me lighten my teaching load so I could write.

And thanks especially to my family for being unfailingly supportive: my best friend and greatest love, Noelle, and our children—Lea, Gerard, Peregrine, Elizabeth, and Aquinnah. You have all kept me going when it seemed overwhelming.

Thank you to my friends and colleagues who took me seriously for so many preposterous-seeming years: Susan Lawler, Matthew Neumann, Dean Dakolias, Mike McGovern, Pat Butler, Mike English, Laura Nooney, Sue Seo, Owen Davis, Jeanne Neumann, Ann Neumann, Roger Ehrenberg, Chris Wiggins, Josh Reich, Greg Yardley, and Vaughn Tan.

I'd also like to thank a few long-ago mentors for teaching me how to think on my feet when things went pear-shaped: Felice Kincannon, John Wren, Randy Weisenberger, and Seth Lemler. We went through some shit together, and watching you so deftly navigate it made me realize I could too.

GLOSSARY

Acquihire: When a startup is acquired by a larger company primarily for its talent, usually engineers. Acquihires are a great way for a startup to save face instead of shutting down: Have another company hire most of the engineers as a package deal and announce to the world that they were "acquired."

AE (account executive): Salesperson in charge of finding customers, closing deals, and maintaining the customer relationship after the sale.

AngelList: A website that lists startups raising money so angel investors can find and invest in them.

ARR: a. Recurring revenue generated by annualized subscriptions (annual recurring revenue); or b. Latest monthly revenue multiplied by twelve (annualized run rate).

B2B (business-to-business): A software or service sold by a business directly to another business. Contrast to, among many other increasingly confusing startup acronyms, B2C, where businesses sell to consumers; D2C, where businesses sell direct to consumers (as opposed to selling through a retailer or wholesaler); and

B2B2C, where businesses sell to another business that sells to the consumer (but where the first business becomes valuable to the consumer in itself; e.g., Microsoft selling Windows through PC manufacturers).

Board deck: A presentation used to update board members on company progress in board meetings.

Board meetings: A regular meeting of the board of directors to hear from company management about the state of the business and to discuss and decide any actions that need to be taken.

Breakup clause: A term in a contract, typically an *LOI* (see), in which the issuer must pay a fee if they decide not to close the deal without good (as specified in the LOI) reason.

Call option: The right, but not the obligation, to acquire equity at a specific price at some point in the future. VCs often say an early-stage investment is a "call option" because it gives them the chance to participate in a future financing if the company becomes hot, even though this is a bit of a misnomer because there is no set price for the future purchase.

Capital calls: When a venture capital firm raises a fund, their investors commit the capital. That is, they agree they will invest a certain amount of money over the life of the fund as needed. But they send the money when the fund needs it, not all at once. A capital call is when the fund asks its investors to wire their share of the money needed to make an investment.

Cap (capitalization) table: A record of who owns or has the option to own what types and amounts of shares in a startup.

Cause: A list of reasons that an executive or founder can be fired without triggering severance payments or other contractual requirements.

COGS (cost of goods sold): Direct costs associated with building a product. Excludes marketing, sales, and distribution, while including delivery costs (e.g., server costs).

Common stock: Your vanilla, no-frills stock, typically owned by founders and employees. Common has fewer rights than the *Preferred stock* (see) purchased by investors.

Corp Dev (corporate development): Team in charge of finding ways for a company to grow outside of their usual sales channels.

Corporate (venture) arms: A division at a large company that makes venture capital investments.

Co-sale right, exempt from the ROFR: An exemption in the IRA (see box in chapter 3) in which certain employees, typically founders, have the right to sell some percentage of their holdings without being subject to the ROFR. This allows founders, who might be rich on paper—they own a large stake in a very valuable company—but cash-poor, to take money off the table.

Crunchbase: An online database of startups and funding rounds.

Decacorns: In 2013, venture capitalist Aileen Lee coined the term unicorn to describe private venture capital–backed companies valued at more than $1 billion. The word unicorn was meant to denote how rare these beautiful creatures were. In the ensuing ten years, as everyone and their dentist poured money into VC, unicorns became so common that VCs couldn't even brag about them anymore. In response, they coined a more impressive word: decacorn. A decacorn is ten times a unicorn, a private company valued at more than $10 billion.

Direct-to-consumer/business-to-consumer (D2C/B2C): See *B2B*.

D&O (Directors & Officers) insurance: Insurance purchased to indemnify a company's board of directors against lawsuits.

Down round: A financing round that occurs at a lower valuation than the previous one. Usually an indication that either something has gone drastically wrong at the company or that the market has tanked. Down rounds can cause excess dilution for founders and early investors leading to bad blood, so many VCs would prefer to not invest at all rather than lead a down round.

Escrow: The holding of money or signatures while a deal is in the process of closing (typically by lawyers). This allows the synchronization of all signatures and sendings of money so no weird legal gaps can open where a deal has been agreed to by some but not all parties or where a deal has been agreed to but money hasn't been wired. It's easier than trying to get everyone to do everything all at the same time.

Exited/exits: When a startup's shareholders have a chance to sell their equity for either cash or more liquid equity. This may take the form of an acquisition (see *M&A*) or an *IPO* (see).

Follow-on round: Any subsequent round that an investor invests in.

Form D: A notice filed with the SEC on the event of a stock offering for sale that includes basic information about the company, its executives, and the size and date of the sale.

Fund expenses: The costs of running the VC firm itself (rent, salaries, phones and computers, etc.).

Good Reason: A list of reasons an executive or founder can quit while still retaining their severance and other benefits. "Good Reason" tries to codify what being fired without actually being fired is: having your compensation reduced, your job description substantially changed for the worse, your responsibilities or direct reports taken away, etc.

Greater fool theory: If you buy something for $100 and then realize it is worth only $90, you are a fool. But you can save your own ass by finding a greater fool and selling it to them for $120. When you are selling something, your goal is to find the greatest fool (see *Winner's curse*). The greatest fool of all is usually the general public, so selling to them in an *IPO* (see) is the best exit of all.

Hacker News: A social news aggregation website run by *Y Combinator* (see). The audience is primarily software engineers and startup folk of the technical bent, so the upvoted articles are usually things of interest to them.

Hockey stick: Also known as "up and to the right," hockey stick growth is when revenue suddenly starts to grow rapidly after a period of low or no growth. When you forecast hockey stick revenue in your board deck, the chart kind of looks like a, you know, hockey stick.

Inside round: When a new round is financed entirely by people who are already investors. Often a really good or a really bad sign.

IPO (initial public offering): When a company lists on a stock market in order to raise money from the public and to create liquidity for its existing shareholders. IPOs are usually the most lucrative exit for the investors and, unlike most acquisitions, leave the current management in charge of the company.

Lead (investor): The VC in a round that issues terms, hires lawyers, and negotiates contracts. It's often the same VC that invests the largest amount of money in the round and sits on the startup's board afterward, but not always.

LOI (letter of intent): A written indication from a potential acquirer of their intent to buy a company and an outline of what the deal would be. While getting something in writing is a huge step in an acquisition process, an LOI is a *nonbinding* (see) offer and the price is liable to change as the acquirer does due diligence. Some LOIs may come with a *breakup clause* (see).

LP (limited partner): One of the investors in a venture capital fund.

M&A (mergers and acquisitions): Companies team up to have a bigger market presence or to use each other's assets. The term acquisition is usually used when one company is buying the other and the acquired company will have little say at the executive level. Merger tends to mean something mutual and friendlier. The friendliest is a merger of equals where the two companies will evenly share ownership and control after the transaction. In reality, every M&A deal is an acquisition to some extent. You can usually tell by seeing which company's CEO ends up being CEO of the combination.

Merger of equals: See *M&A*.

Milestone: A tangible event (working software, first users, paying customers, etc.) that shows that a startup is making progress toward being a real company.

Moats: A colloquial term for a sustainable competitive advantage. A way to make it harder for imitators to compete with you. A moat might be increasing returns to scale, network effects, a well-known brand, patents, etc.

MRR (monthly recurring revenue): Predictable, monthly revenue generated by subscriptions.

NDA (non-disclosure agreement): A legal agreement between a company and another person (employee, contractor) that prohibits that person from sharing sensitive company information, even after they are no longer employed by the company.

Nonbinding: An offer or agreement that doesn't come with a contractual obligation to complete it.

NVCA (National Venture Capital Association): A trade association formed primarily to lobby on behalf of venture capital firms but that also provides some assistance to members, such as model legal documents and industry research.

Participating preferred: A type of *Preferred stock* (see) that not only returns the investors' money before paying anything to Common shareholders, but requires the Preferred investors to *make* a multiple of their investment before the Common makes anything.

Partner: One of the owners of a venture capital fund (versus, say, associates, who are mere employees). It is almost always the partners who decide which startups to invest in and who manage the investment afterward.

PE (private equity) funds: A fund that invests in companies that are not traded on a stock exchange. This includes both venture capital funds and funds that invest in more mature businesses, like some buyout and hedge funds.

PLG (product-led growth): Most products must be sold. Product-led growth is the idea that some products sell themselves. Building a product that customers just show up to buy is the field of dreams in the startup world but, like the *Field of Dreams*, it's rarely anything but wishful thinking.

Post-money valuation: See *pre-money/post-money valuation.*

Preferred stock: Class of stock typically reserved for investors, which comes with special privileges, most notably that the Preferred stock gets paid first in any sale or liquidation of the company. For example, if the company has raised $100 million through sales of preferred stock but later doesn't do as well as expected and is sold for a total of $50 million, then the preferred stockholders get the entire $50 million and the Common stockholders (including the founders and employees) get nothing. Preferred stock is a necessary protection for VCs when the *pre-money valuation* (see) does not reflect what the company could be sold for, which is almost always the case in VC.

Pre-money/post-money valuation: Notionally, a startup's value immediately before and after a round of financing. The pre-money is the number of shares in the company before the financing multiplied by the price per share offered in the financing. The post-money is the number of shares after the financing multiplied by the price per share. Theoretically, the post-money valuation is the pre-money valuation plus the amount of money invested in the round, but this often isn't exactly true because the financing may also require the option pool being expanded, etc.

Product market fit: The semi-mystical moment when a company's product perfectly suits their customer, so that customers begin clamoring to buy it. While startup growth gurus say you'll know this moment when it happens, it more often seems that people only recognize it several years later, when they retroactively try to claim that their success was a result of them knowing exactly what they were doing.

Recycle: When a venture fund takes the money from an exit and invests it back into a new startup instead of returning it to their limited partners. This is a way to increase the size of their fund and thus the overall amount of money they can make. For instance, if a VC raises a $100 million fund, but has an exit in year three of $20 million, they may recycle that $20 million by investing it in more startups. They have, in effect, turned their $100 million fund into a $120 million fund.

Retained search: Also called headhunting, where recruiters are hired, typically for a flat fee, partly paid up front and partly paid on successful completion, to find and hire an executive. This is in contrast to a contingent search in which the recruiters are paid only after someone is actually hired. Although the payment may be similar in the end, contingent search firms have an incentive to find a spot for a person while retained search firms are motivated to find a person to fill a spot.

Return on Investment (ROI): The gain on an investment divided by its cost.

RIA (registered investment advisor): In the USA, venture capital firms are exempt from reporting requirements that most other investment firms have to follow. But when more money pours into venture than VCs know how to spend, they decide to make non-venture investments. To be allowed to do so, they must become RIAs. In the 2020s, these non-venture investments were in crypto, other venture funds, and public market equities. In the 1980s, they were in leveraged buyouts. Generally, when venture firms decide they would rather put their money in non-venture investments, it means that either venture prices are too high or expected exits are too low.

SaaS (software-as-a-service): Software licensed and centrally hosted instead of the older "shrinkwrap" model, where software was sold to a customer who then had to install it on their own computers, then make sure the computers stayed up and someone kept the software updated. Once internet connections became ubiquitous and reliable, it just made sense to customers to have the software provider do these things. And it made sense to the software provider because they could now charge a subscription instead of a one-time fee.

Shiva: Traditional Jewish gathering to mourn someone who has died.

Single/double trigger acceleration: Startup stock options vest over time: Someone may be given options on ten thousand shares of stock vesting over five years. This means (though it may be more complicated) that they have the right to two thousand options each year for five years. But if the company is acquired by another company or the option holder is fired, that vesting stops. Executives may negotiate their employment contracts with clauses that allow all of their options to vest immediately if some event occurs, like an acquisition, being fired without *cause* (see), or quitting for *Good Reason* (see). Single-trigger acceleration usually means that the employee becomes fully vested if the company is acquired. Double-trigger means the employee becomes vested if an acquisition happens and then the employee is terminated or leaves for Good Reason.

Stock option pool: Options on shares of *common stock* (see) reserved to be granted over time to employees as an incentive for them to make the company more valuable.

Strategic: A company who would have a strategic interest in a startup. Strategics are sometimes approached to invest in a startup and often do. They also are often the acquirers of the startup.

Syndicate: Many venture financings include more than one investor, either because no single investor has enough money to fund the whole round themselves, or because different investors bring different expertise to the startup. This group of investors is called a syndicate. When a VC finds an investment they want to make and brings other investors in to invest as well, they are syndicating the deal.

TAM (total addressable market): Theoretical maximum amount of the market a company could capture if everyone who could use the product bought from that company.

Thesis: A thesis is a venture capitalist's elevator pitch of what they plan to invest in. It usually includes an area (or a few areas) of specialization and the VC's prediction of why those markets are The Future.

Tier 1/2 firm: A top venture capital firm (e.g., Accel Partners, Andreessen Horowitz, etc.). There are thousands of active venture capital firms, and if you listen to them, they are all among the top firms. Because returns are not public, there's no real way of knowing for sure, so which firms are Tier 1, Tier 2, or below is more folk wisdom than fact.

Triple-double/triple-triple-double-double: The VC expectation of revenue growth in early-stage *SaaS* (see) companies. Revenue triples for two consecutive years, and then doubles each of the following two years. This expectation is rarely met.

Use of funds: The slide a startup shows when a VC asks, "What are you going to do with my money?" even though the answer is almost always "Hire people."

Winner's curse: By definition, the winner of an auction is the one who paid more than anyone else was willing to. Since they can't sell for as much as they paid, they have paid more than the item is worth. This means that the winner of any auction has *always* overpaid (unless they know something everyone else doesn't know, and this information is revealed after the auction).

Y Combinator: A notable and influential startup incubator/accelerator. Named after an obscure and rarely used programming construct.

ABOUT THE AUTHORS

Elizabeth Zalman is an infrastructure and information security expert. She is a two-time founder/CEO of venture-backed companies, building the first to a successful exit and the second to a multi-hundred-million-dollar business. Liz has raised more than $100 million in venture capital from the most renowned investors in the world. She is also a frequent speaker and guest for industry events and tech podcasts, in addition to being an investor and advisor herself.

A twenty-five year veteran of venture capital, **Jerry Neumann** has invested in some of the most successful venture-funded companies of the past three decades and has worked alongside dozens of entrepreneurs as investor, board member, and advisor. He has been named one of the "100 best early-stage investors" and one of the "most important VCs in New York" by *Business Insider*. Jerry also teaches entrepreneurship at Columbia University.